UITGAVEN VAN HET
NEDERLANDS HISTORISCH-ARCHAEOLOGISCH INSTITUUT TE ISTANBUL

Publications de l'Institut historique et archéologique néerlandais de Stamboul

sous la direction de
A. A. CENSE et A. A. KAMPMAN

VIII

# A DECADE
# OF ARCHAEOLOGY IN ISRAEL
## 1948—1958

# A DECADE
# OF ARCHAEOLOGY IN ISRAEL

## 1948-1958

BY

## Sh. YEIVIN

İSTANBUL
NEDERLANDS HISTORISCH-ARCHAEOLOGISCH INSTITUUT
IN HET NABIJE OOSTEN
1960

Copyright 1960 by
Nederlands Historisch-Archaeologisch Instituut in het Nabije Oosten
Noordeindsplein 4a, Leiden

Printed in the Netherlands

# TABLE OF CONTENTS

PLATES

*Plate I.*

1. The Restored Façade of the Catacomb of Sarcophagi at Bet-She'arim.
   (By kindness of Dr. N. Avigad, Director of the IES's Expedition to Bet-She'arim).
2. Male Bone Statuette from the Chalcolithic Site of Be'er Zafad, near Beersheba.
   (By kindness of M. J. Perrot, Director of the CNRS's Expedition to Be'er Zafad).
3. A Set of Three Basalt Bowls from Be'er Matar.

*Plate II.*

1. A Chalcolithic Clay Ossuary from 'Azor, in the Shape of a Two-Storeyed Building.
2. A Group of Chalcolithic Stone-Vases from Kabri.
3. A Basalt Paved Street in an EC Stratum at Bet-Yerah (South).

*Plate III.*

1. A Modern Cast from an Ancient Mould of a Statuette of 'Atrat-Yam (?) from Nehariyya.
2. A Basalt Lion Orthostat from the Doorway of the Northern LC Temple at Hazor.
   (By kindness of Dr. Y. Yadin, Director of the James de Rothschild's Expedition to Hazor).
3. A Fragment of a Sandstone Doorjamb from the LC Gateway at Jaffa inscribed with the Titles of Ramses II.
   (By kindness of the Municipality of Tel-Aviv and Dr. Y. Kaplan, the Director of the Excavations).
4. A Terracotta Figurine from the LI (Persian) Temple near Tell Makmish.

*Plate IV.*

1. The Gateway of the Acropolis at Tel "Gat" in Stratum VIII.
   (IXth century B.C.E.) Inside the city.
2. One of the Semi-Detached Columns and Capitals from the Structure on the Lowest Terrace of Herod's Palace at Masada. (Photograph A. Volk.)

# FIGURES IN TEXT

1. Map of excavated sites in Israel. (pp. 4 and 5).

2. A Grafitto Representation of a Naval Battle from a Hasmonean Tomb at Jerusalem.

3. Plan of the Large "Sarcophagi" Catacomb at Bet-She'arim. (p. 6).

4. Plan and Arrangement of Funerary Equipment in An EC Tomb at Hazzorea'. (p. 9).

5. Sketch-Map of Tel Bet-Yerah Showing Various Areas of Excavations and the Hellenistic Fortifications. (p. 20).

6. Sketch-map of Hazor (tell and enclosure) showing the Various Excavated Areas. (By kindness of Dr. Y. Yadin, Director of the James de Rothschilds' Expedition). (p. 23).

7. Plan of a Caravanserai (?) of the IXth Century B.C.E., East of Tel Hazor. (p. 27).

8. Sketch-map of the So-called Tel "Gat", Showing the Various Excavated Areas. (p. 29).

9. Plan of Stratum X (XIth–Xth centuries B.C.E.) at el-Khirbe (Qasile) Showing Two Rows of "Four-Spaced" Buildings. (By kindness of Dr. B. Mazar, director of the IES Expedition to El-Khirbeh-Qasile). (p. 24)

# ABBREVIATIONS

For abbreviations of archaeological periods see table on pp. XII–XIII.

| | | |
|---|---|---|
| AAA | = | Liverpool Annals of Archaeology and Anthropology. |
| 'Alon | = | 'Alon Mahleqet (later: 'Agaf) Ha'atiqot (Bulletin of the Division (later: Department) of Antiquities), Hebrew. |
| 'Atiqot | = | (Antiquities), Journal of the Israel Department of Antiquities, Hebrew and English or French. |
| BASOR | = | Bulletin of the American Schools of Oriental Research. |
| B.C.E. | = | Before Christian Era. |
| BIES | = | Bulletin of the Israel Exploration Society, Hebrew. |
| BJPES | = | Bulletin of the Jewish Palestine Exploration Society, later = BIES. |
| C.E. | = | Christian Era. |
| EI | = | Eretz-Israel, Annual of the Israel Exploration Society, Hebrew. |
| IEJ | = | Israel Exploration Journal. |
| IES | = | Israel Exploration Society. |
| ME | = | Middle East. |
| PEF | = | Palestine Exploration Fund. |
| QDAP | = | Quarterly of the Department of Antiquities, Palestine. |
| RB | = | Revue Biblique. |

## ARCHAEOLOGICAL AND HISTORICAL PERIODS IN ISRAEL

### Stone Age

| | | |
|---|---|---|
| Palaeolithic | beginning about 250,000 B.C.E. | |
| Mesolithic | beginning about 10,000 B.C.E. | |
| Neolithic { prepottery | beginning about 7,000 B.C.E. | |
|          { pottery | beginning about 5,000 B.C.E. | |

### Chalcolithic Period

about 4,000–3,200 B.C.E.

### Canaanite Period (Bronze Age)

| | | |
|---|---|---|
| EC = Early Canaanite,   phase I | about 3,200–2,900 B.C.E. | |
|                phase II | about 2,900–2,600 B.C.E. | |
|                phase III–IV | about 2,600–2,200 B.C.E. | |
| Intermediate, EC – MC | about 2,200–1,950 B.C.E. | |
| MC = Middle Canaanite, phase I | about 1,950–1,750 B.C.E. | } Age of the Patriarchs |
|                 phase II | about 1,750–1,550 B.C.E. | |
| LC = Late Canaanite,   phase I | about 1,550–1,380 B.C.E. | Egyptian Domination (about 1465–1140 B.C.E.) |
|                 phase II | about 1,380–1,180 B.C.E. | The Israelite Conquest |

### Israelite Period (Iron Age)

| | | |
|---|---|---|
| Israelite I (= EI = Early Israelite),   phase I | about 1,180–1,050 B.C.E. | Period of the Judges |
|            phase II | about 1,050– 970 B.C.E. | Saul (ab. 1,017–1,006 B.C.E.) and David (ab. 1,006–967 B.C.E.) |
| Israelite II (= MI = Middle Israelite, phase I ) | about 970– 840 B.C.E. | Solomon (ab. 970–940 B.C.E.) Juda and Israel till Jehu's restoration (841 B.C.E.) |
| Israelite III (= MI = Middle Israelite, phase II) | about 840– 580 B.C.E. | Juda and Israel till the capture of Jerusalem (586 B.C.E.) |
| Israelite IV (= LI = Late Israelite) | about 580– 330 B.C.E. | Neo-Babylonian and Persian Domination till the Macedonian Conquest (332 B.C.E.) |

### Hellenistic Period

about 330– 165 B.C.E.      The "Great Assembly" till the Hasmonean revolt

| Period | Date | Description |
|---|---|---|
| *Roman Period* | | |
| Roman I | about 70– 135 C.E. | The Early Tannaim till the death of Bar-Kokheba (135 C.E.) |
| Roman II | about 135– 330 C.E. | The Late Tannaim and Early Amoraim |
| *Byzantine Period* | | |
| Byzantine I | about 330– 395 C.E. | The Late Amoraim till the codification of the Jerusalemite Talmud (425 C.E.) |
| Byzantine II | about 395– 640 C.E. | The Sevoraim |
| *Islamic Period I* | | |
| Islamic Ia | 640– 750 C.E. | Islamic conquest and 'Umayyad Dynasty |
| Islamic Ib | 750– 850 C.E. | 'Abbasid Dynasty |
| Islamic Ic | 850–1073 C.E. | Petty Dynasties (850–1073 C.E.) Seldjuk Dynasty (1073–1194 C.E.) |
| Crusaders' Period | 1099–1291 C.E. | |
| Islamic Period II | 1290–1517 C.E. | Mamluk Dynasties |
| Islamic Period III | 1517 C.E. | Ottoman conquest |
| *End of archaeological periods* | 1700 C.E. | |

# A DECADE OF ARCHAEOLOGICAL ACTIVITY
# IN ISRAEL (1948-1958)

## I. *Introduction*

The Department of Antiquities was founded on July 27, 1948, shortly after the establishment of the State of Israel. It was a difficult time for archaeology. The offices of the Mandatory Government Department of Antiquities and its Museum building were situated in the Jordanian part of Jerusalem. The new State of Israel possessed neither exhibits nor administrative and archaeological files. It did not possess an archaeological library or a collection of photographs, maps and plans. All foreign archaeological institutions, with the exception of the Pontifical Biblical Institute, were also situated in Jordan territory; while the library and collections of the Hebrew University Department of Archaeology and the attached Museum of Jewish Antiquities, housed on Mount Scopus, were inaccessible for purposes of study and research. Such material as the Israel Exploration Society possessed was deposited in the Hebrew University Department of Archaeology on Mount Scopus, or in the store-rooms and laboratories of the Palestine Archaeological Museum belonging to the Mandatory Government.

The Jewish staff of the Mandatory Department of Antiquities, helped by new academic and administrative members, set to work immediately on the difficult task of both organizing the current administrative work of the Department and renewing its scientific activities. They established a new library, collected exhibits, and made auxiliary collections of photographs, maps and bibliographical material. The work of the Department expanded and with it grew the staff. There were only eleven employees on the staff in July 1948. Now, including guards, the staff comprises fifty-six permanent, and fourteen part-time, or temporary workers.

The Department of Antiquities consists of six divisions: Inspectorate, Conservation of Monuments, Archaeological Survey and Excavations, Museum, Archaeological Archives and Library, Research Secretariat (research and publications). An attempt was made to enlist the aid of those members of the general public who were interested in knowing more about the country's past and its antiquities, in spreading this knowledge, and in cultivating a positive attitude toward the relics of the past. The Department sought such amateurs in every part of the country. Wherever they were found, one, two, or three of them (in accordance with the size of the locality and the number of those interested) were appointed Trustees of the

Association of Friends of Antiquities, an organization which connects all the Trustees with the Department of Antiquities. 173 trustees have so far been appointed in 140 towns and settlements. The campaign to expand this Association continues, for the value of its activities is incalculable. Much of the Department's varied work has been carried out as a result of information concerning discoveries and remains which Trustees from all parts of the country have communicated. The Trustees, for their part, have had a chance to receive guidance from experts on a subject which interests them, and have been given a number of courses on special aspects of the archaeology of this country[1]).

In addition, two types of guards have been appointed. There are now local guards at isolated sites or monuments, and regional guards in charge of a group of sites or monuments, within a larger area. The regional guards assist the Zonal Inspectors in their routine duties, and also occasionally carry out small soundings and exploratory digs on their own responsibility. The guards form a special unit under the command of the Chief Guard.

At the same time, non-government bodies interested in archaeology renewed and continued to expand their activities. The Hebrew University expanded its Institute of Archaeology, comprising now a teaching staff of seven. This Institute has carried out several excavations,[2]) partly on its own, and partly in cooperation with other archaeological bodies in Israel, and was also co-sponsor of the Joint Expedition to Hazor.

The Israel Exploration Society has continuously enlarged its registered membership both in the country and abroad (at present 1500 and 200 resp.). It sponsored a series of excavations both on its own, as well as in cooperation with other bodies[3]), maintained its periodical publications and added to them[4]), and continued with its annual conferences for the interested public, which convene during the „middle-days" of the Feast of Tabernacles and are attended by over 1000 persons, a sure sign of the very keen and active interest in archaeology among large sections of the public, and especially the younger generation.

## II. *Excavations: General*

The Division of Archaeological Survey and Excavations became the most active of the Department of Antiquities' Divisions. Even though the Department of Antiquities attempted from the start to work out long-term plans for this Division, the exigencies of the day-to-day work ruined most of them, for the Department was forced to submit to the urgent demands made on it by numerous development schemes, which could not be postponed. In all these activities the Department received financial and moral support from local authorities in whose districts

---

[1]) See below, p. 58.   [2]) See below, pp. 47–49.   [3]) See below, pp. 47–49.   [4]) See below, pp. 56 ff.

soundings and excavations were carried out, as well as from Government institutions and public organizations which planned and executed the various development works leading to such soundings. Help was also received from private individuals on whose property remains requiring examination were found.

In the course of time a clear picture began to emerge from these random and varied soundings and exploratory excavations, which were the chief activity of the Division. Some of these digs, which started as emergency explorations, turned in the course of time, into large scale investigations of first-rate importance, carried on for several consecutive seasons.[5]

All in all some 320 large-scale operations and small soundings were carried out by the Department (including such as were undertaken in collaboration with other bodies) in the course of the last decade (1948–1958). These may be divided into five main groups: (a) the clearing of individual graves and cemeteries; (b) the beginnings of human life in this country: the Early and Middle Stone Ages; the start of civilization in the Late Stone Age, and the transition to the use of metals of the Chalcolithic cultures; the EC[6] period of the Early Bronze cultures; (c) the Canaanite Period[7]; (d) the Israelite Period[8]; (e) the late periods especially of Roman and Byzantine domination which preceded the Arab conquest (fig. 1).

## III. *Excavations: Tombs*

A large proportion of the investigations concerned with group (a) were individual graves or isolated tomb-caves from the first century B.C.E. to the Arab conquest. This is not really surprising, as during that period, particularly in the latter part of it, the country was more densely populated than at any other time in its history. A Hellenistic cemetery uncovered at Acre, and excavated on behalf of the Depart-

---

[5] See below, pp. 17; 19–20; 34–35; 40 ff.

[6] For the abbreviations used here see the table on pp. XII–XIII.

[7] See below, pp. 19 ff.

[8] The Israel Department of Antiquities reintroduced into use the chronological classification proposed in 1922, *RB* 32 (1923), pp. 272 ff., which established historico-cultural terms for the various stages of the development of civilization in this country. Such terms as are used in European Prehistory (Bronze and Iron Ages) are so-far irreplaceable there, since the periods in question cannot be correlated to definite historical events or closely definable general ethnic groups. In Israel, on the other hand, such historical and ethnic associations do exist, and are preferable to vague and inexpressive terms.

This does not mean that the term Canaanite figures here in any precise connotation; it is used within its general meaning in the Bible: the pre-Israelite stratum of civilization in this country. For a recent attempt to subdivide the Israelite period further see Y. Aharoni and Ruth Amiran, IEJ VII (1958), pp. 171 ff.

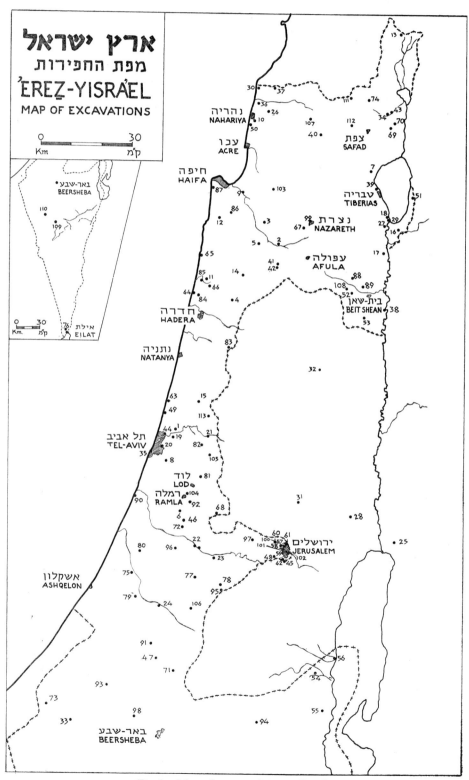

Fig. 1.   Map of excavated sites in Israel.

On this map are marked only such excavated or restored sites as are mentioned in the text.

1) Ḥorvat Ḥadra
2) Kefar Barukh
3) Bet-She'arim
4) Tell el-'Asawir
5) Hazzorea'
6) Na'an
7) Ginnosar
8) 'Azor
9) Tell 'Abu Hawam
10) 'Evron
11) Kabara Cave
12) 'Oren Cave
13) Ma'ayan Barukh
14) Gal'ed
15) Zofit
16) Sha'ar Haggolan
17) Gesher
18) Kinneret (village)
19) Bene Braq
20) Giv'ataim
21) Aphek – Rosh Ha'ayin
22) Teluliot Battish
23) Bet-Shemesh
24) Tel "Gat" (Tell el-'Areyni)
25) Tuleylat Ghasul
26) Kabrit (Kabri)
27) Tel 'Ely (Kh. Sheykh 'Aly)
28) Jericho (Tell es-Sultan)
29) Bet-Yerah (Kh. Kerak)
30) Rosh Hanniqra (Kh. et-Taba'iq)
31) 'Ay
32) Tell el-Fari'a (north)
33) Sharuhen (Tell el-Fari'a, south)
34) Hazor
35) Tel Jaffa
36) Gesher Hazziv
37) Hanita
38) Kefar Ruppin
39) Tel Raqqat (Tell el-Quneytra)
40) Tel Harashim (Kh. et-Tuleyl)
41) Megiddo (historical site)
42) Megiddo (the collective settlement)

43) Ayyelet Hashshahar
44) el-Khirbe (Qasile)
45) Ramat Rahel
46) Tell Malat
47) Tel Milha
48) Manahat
49) Tell Makmish
50) Shave Zion (Nea Kome)
51) Susita (Hippos)
52) 'Eyn Shoqeq
53) Farwana
54) Valley of Hever (Wadi Habra)
55) Massada
56) 'Eyn-Gedi
57) Church of St.-George at Giv'at Ram
58) The Nymphaeum within the precincts of the Qirya
59) The Nymphaeum west of the Valley of the Cross
60) The Small Fort on Mount Menuhot (Ras el-'Alawi)
61) The Group of Sanhedriyya Tombs
62) Funerary Chapel near Bet-Safafa
63) Rishpon (Apollonia)
64) Caesarea (Maritima)
65) Dor (Dora)
66) Binyemina
67) Yafia'
68) Sha'albim
69) Horvat Shura
70) Horvat Nator
71) Horvat Migdal Ziqlag
72) Kh. er-Ruqqadiyye
73) Horvat Ma'on
74) 'Alma
75) Massu'ot Yizhaq
76) Remains of a Byzantine Village in the Valley of Roded
77) 'Agur
78) Roglit (Kh. Jurfa)
79) Ozem
80) Hazor, south (Kh. Banaya)

81) Kefar Truman
82) Kefar Syrkin
83) Bahan
84) Church in Byzantine Cemetery near Caesarea
85) Church on the Crocodilion River
86) Kh. Damun (in the Carmel Range)
87) Remains of a Monastery at Sha'ar Ha'aliyya (Haifa)
88) Bet Hashshitta
89) Sede Nahum
90) Yavne-Yam
91) Tel Nagila
92) Ras Abu Humeyd
93) Tel Haror
94) Tel 'Arad
95) 'Adullam
96) Tell Muqanna'
97) Qaryet el-'Inab
98) Be'er Raqiq
99) The Church of Announciation at Nazareth
100) Iason's Mausoleum in Alfassi St., Jerusalem
101) The Mausoleum of King Herod's Family at Jerusalem
101) Church on Mount John the High Priest, Jerusalem
103) Shefar'am
104) Bi'r Zeybak
105) Mazor
106) Bet-Govrin
107) Sukhmata
108) Bet-Alpha
109) 'Avdat
110) Shivta
111) Kefar Bir'am
112) Meron
113) Jaljuliyye

ment by Mrs. Ruth Amiran, showed five types of burial, evidently belonging to different phases within that period. Some of the finds exhibit rather interesting local art traditions.[9])

Two tombs uncovered in different quarters of Jerusalem contained ossuaries, one bearing the name: Yuda; the other: Rufus who is Daniel. The excavation of the first was directed by Dr. I. Ben-Dor; the excavation of the second by Dr. Y. Aharoni. A combination of Hebrew and Greek names for the same person has been noted before in the Midrashim and in the Bet-She'arim cemetery of the IIIrd and IVth centuries C.E. The Greek inscriptions above, however, belong to an earlier period (Ist. cent. B.C.E. – Ist cent. C.E.). For the first time Jewish stone ossuaries were discovered outside the mountainous area of the country both in the maritime plain near Tel-Aviv (Dr. J. Kaplan's excavation on behalf of the Department at Shikkun Dan, Ḥorvat Hadar) and in the Megiddo Plain (Dr. Z. Goldman's dig on behalf of the Department at Kefar Barukh). These date probably to the IInd-IIIrd centuries C.E. New light was also thrown on the history of the development of the glass industry in this country. Rare and isolated vessels begin to appear at the end of the Israelite period, as e.g., in a LI grave at Bet-She'an. In the Hellenistic period, glass vessels are still comparatively rare. They become more or less common only in the Herodian period. The large scale production of glassware of all types – glasses, bowls, plates, *unguaria*, jars and bottles – only reached its height at the end of the IIIrd cent. C.E. A similar process of industrialization apparently marks the mass production of pottery lamps, of fixed yet varied types.

A monumental rock-hewn family tomb of the Hasmonean period (late IInd – early Ist cent. B.C.E.) was accidentally uncovered in Alfasi St. at Jerusalem, and investigated on behalf of the Department by Messrs. M. Dothan and L. Y. Rahmani. Apart from the monumental approach and unusual portico supported in front on only one column in the middle, between two antae, it contained a large plain rock-hewn chamber entered by a small doorway at the back (north) of the portico, and another smaller two storied room with *kokhim* (burial niches) in one of the side walls (west). On the plastered walls of the portico were funerary inscriptions in Aramaic and Greek, and a naval battle scene between a merchantman escorted by a small war-galley and a larger man of war (fig. 2) all done in charcoal (?). The tomb was reused for later burials towards the middle of the Ist cent. C.E., and later largely destroyed and covered up by debris as a result of an ancient earthquake[10]). Of especial interest, both as monumental remains, as well as new and illuminating discoveries for the history of the period and its Jewish art, are the last five campaigns of excavations conducted by the Israel Exploration Society at Bet-She'arim

---

[9]) Ruth Amiran, 'Alon 3 (June 1951), p. 45.

[10]) For a detailed report, and the implications of this and other smaller contemporaneous tombs round Jerusalem see L. Y. Rahmani's forthcoming article in 'Atiqot III.

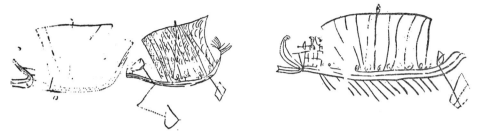

Fig. 2.   A Grafitto Representation of a Naval Battle from a Hasmonean Tomb at Jerusalem

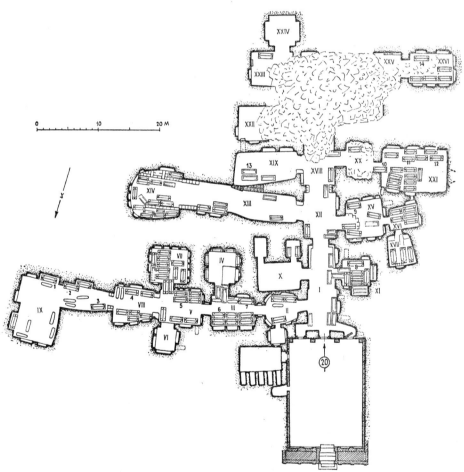

Fig. 3.   Plan of the Large "Sarcophagi" Catacomb at Bet-She'arim.

(cf. fig. 1)[11]). Four of these campaigns were directed by Prof. N. Avigad, mainly in the necropolis, while one (1956) was led by Prof. B. Mazar and conducted mainly in the mound of the ancient city.

Here were found remains of two large public buildings. One was of the usual basilica type, oriented east-west, which may have been a *Bet-Wa'ad* (study hall of the sages). The nature of the other could not be established, since but little of it has survived, namely a flight of broad steps constituting the approach to its northern façade and a massive threshold to a broad and monumental entrance. The most surprising result of the investigation of this part of the mound was the great extension of the span of life of this settlement, as revealed there. A trial pit sunk by Mazar proved that the earliest occupation of the site belongs to the days of the Israelite Monarchy, continuing – on that spot – till the IVth century C.E. almost without a break; while a short examination by Avigad of some remains down the slope on the northern edge of the tell uncovered remains of a large installation for extracting olive oil connected with a dwelling house of the VIth-VIIth cent. C.E. This proves that after its destruction in the so-called „Gallus Revolt" (352 C.E.) the town was resettled and continued in occupation till the Early Arab period.

In the necropolis, on the lower northern slope of the natural hill on which the tell is situated, were unearthed several new catacombs. Most of them conformed in plan, type and arrangement to those excavated previously[12]). However, two proved to be exceptionally monumental, with large partly built-up courtyards, and upper façades (ashlar masonry), three arched-over entrances in the façade, and originally paved platforms above them, leading to monumental flights of large steps culminating in a central half-rounded niche in each case. In one case the flight of steps was half-rounded in a wide arch; in the other, it rose on three sides of the platform like the letter ⊓ (pl. I, 1). The former funerary monument may possibly be attributed to the patriarchal family of Rabbi *Yehuda hannasi'*, the compiler of the Mishna[13]). The other is by far the largest catacomb yet discovered in this necropolis (fig. 3). It also seems to be the earliest. The part cleared so far is full of limestone sarcophagi, and fragments of some marble ones, many of which are decorated in relief or with incised ornamental motives, showing human busts, animals and birds, façades of houses, or geometric patterns (painted over). Several Hebrew and Aramaic inscriptions were incised or painted on the covers. Other catacombs, too, revealed their share of the Hebrew, Aramaic and Greek inscriptions, identifying a large number of the deceased as having been brought for burial here from Phoenician and Syrian towns. One inscription in what seems to be Pehlevy script has not been deciphered as yet.

---

[11]) For earlier campaigns in 1936–1940 see B. Mazar (Maisler), *Beth She'arim*, 2nd ed., Jerusalem, 1957.

[12]) See above, note 11.

[13]) For details see N. Avigad, IEJ V (1955), pp. 218–226, 236–239.

One so far inexplicable discovery was made within the confines of this necropolis. A large and deep cistern hewn in the rock chock full of absolutely unused and complete glass vessels and terracotta lamps.

Isolated graves of earlier periods have also been unearthed throughout the country. Several were discovered in the course of unearthing relatively large cemeteries.

Thus, a burial ground was discovered near the ancient settlement, not yet identified, represented by Tell el-'Asawir at the entrance to the Valley of 'Iron (Wadi 'Ara). Here under the direction of Dr. Dothan, a tomb-cave was completely excavated, and two layers of mass inhumation uncovered. In the top part of the cave, dug out in the soft *kurkar* (a calcareous limestone), were remains of several burials belonging to the age of the Patriarchs (under Hyksos rule, MC II). Underneath this burial stratum a fairly thick layer of sterile earth was found; and beneath it, at the bottom of the cave, was a heavy accumulation of mass burials, containing hundreds of pots and several stone beads and pendants, all belonging to the period of transition between the Chalcolithic and the EC cultures. This mass grave is of particular interest, because it shows that the bodies were dismembered at the time of interment, since human teeth and finger bones were found in large shallow bowls; and also proves that the late Chalcolithic culture was diffused in the Sharon as well as in the hills of Samaria (the Northern Tell el-Fari'a). It is called the Esdraelon culture after the site of its first discovery at 'Afula, and it is typified by its greenish-grey burnished bowls. It also shows that this late stage in the Chalcolithic cultures is directly connected with the beginnings of the EC civilization, as several small jars characteristic of the first stage of the EC period have been found in this grave.

Small burial grounds of the EC and MC periods were found in the Bet-She'an valley and investigated by Mr. N. Zori; most of them, however, had been disturbed and looted in early times.

An undisturbed grave in a small EC cemetery near Hazzorea' (cf. fig. 1), excavated on behalf of the Department by Mr. E. Anati, showed a very interesting arrangement of funerary equipment and may point to especial funerary rites performed in the burial cave (fig. 4).

Three cemeteries belonging to the Age of the Patriarchs were discovered, one south of the Tel Aviv port on the high *kurkar* ridge near the sea, another near *kibbuz* Na'an, and a third at Ghuweyr 'Abu Shushe, near Ginnosar. The excavation of the first cemetery was directed by Dr. Y. Kaplan; Dr. I. Ben Dor and later Mr. Y. Ory directed the second excavation; while Miss Claire Epstein with Mrs. Ora Negbi conducted the third.

In the cemetery near Ginnosar, only a small part of which was explored (a total of five graves), three contained mass burials apparently exhibiting two stages of inhumation; the second and final, taking place after the decay of the flesh; then, the long and other bones (ribs, toes, fingers, etc.) were heaped up at the bottom of a shallow pit, while the skulls were buried separately in one or two layers above

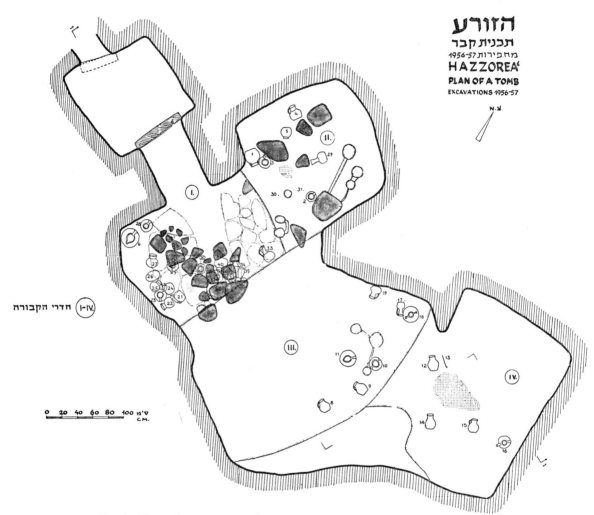

Fig. 4. Plan and Arrangement of Funerary Equipment in An EC Tomb at Hazzorea͑.

I – IV Burial Rooms

such heaps, and with them was placed the major part of the accompanying funerary gifts. In another larger grave, the lowest layer still contained only skulls surrounded by a large deposit of funerary equipment in the middle layer, and several clay lamps both in the middle and top layers[14]).

Another mass grave near 'Azor[15]) contained burials starting with the MC II (Hyksos rule) and ending with the EI I (Philistine rule) period. The Hyksos burials were accompanied by sacrificial interments of horses or asses. The funerary equipment included objects and scarabs. The former were of the usual MC II types, while the scarabs prove quite conclusively that the MC II (Hyksos) culture continued to prosper in Canaan well into the XVIth and possibly the early XVth century B.C.E., as already hinted by finds of the Tel Aviv Harbour cemetery[16]).

Ramblers in the neighbourhood of the Kishon harbour noticed a large number of sherds scattered over a considerable area, even though there were no signs of archaeological debris or architectural remains. When the area was inspected, it was at once thought that these were the remains of the cemetery belonging to the ancient settlement of Tell 'Abu Hawam, which the excavator of the Tell had failed to discover. A thorough investigation on the spot revealed the remains of a cemetery. Wind and rain erosion have destroyed the graves and scattered their contents, leaving only the heavy sherds *in situ*. On one spot only was a group of graves preserved and excavated on behalf of the Department by Mr. E. Anati. Their contents dated them to the LC[17]). At another place in the same area remains of an infant burial of the LI period were excavated by Mr. M. Prausnitz. The Persian period is the last one in the history of the settlement on this spot.

Persistent rumours assigned to 'Azor also an extensive Philistine cemetery; evidence of illicite grave digging on the edges of the hill, on top of which lies a Moslem Arab cemetery, led the Department to undertake an investigation, directed by Dr. M. Dothan. An area free from modern graves on the NE edge of the hill revealed a cemetery containing burials which range from the XIIth to the early IXth centuries B.C.E., later reused by the Crusaders, who greatly disturbed the earlier graves. There were also some indications that prior to its use as a cemetery

---

[14]) Apparently the cemetery was abandoned before the surviving relations had time to perform the second stage of dismembering the bodies; or perhaps no surviving relations were left, who would take care of the performance. There always remains the possibility of chronological or other differences in burial customs. The latter seems to be excluded in this case of a common grave; the former is possible, but is still not very likely within such a short space of time.

[15]) Some 5 kms. south-east of Tel-Aviv, mentioned in the Septuagint (B version) of *Josh*. 19 : 45 (instead of Yehud) as a Danite town, and in the Annals of Sennacherib of Assyria as one of the cities of the king of Ascalon.

[16]) For a preliminary report see IEJ VIII (1958), pp. 272-4. A detailed report will be published in 'Atiqot III, in which will be discussed also comparative material from other sites. – Cf. 'Atiqot I (1955), pp. 18 ff.

[17]) A full report on the LC cemetery in 'Atiqot II (1959), pp. 89 ff.

in the EI period, the site formed part of a Late Canaanite settlement on the spot.
In spite of the small area excavated (some 100 sq.m.) the investigation yielded a
large number of finds, and rich information on commercial contacts with Cyprus
throughout the XIIth – Xth centuries B.C.E., as well as on the burial customs in the
Philistine graves.

## IV. *Excavations: The Stone Age and Beginnings of Civilization*

A second class of exploratory digs included planned or random investigations at
several Stone Age open air stations. Dr. M. Stekelis excavated on behalf of the
Department of Antiquities near 'Evron; investigations were made in the bed of the
Jordan in connection with the Ḥule drainage works. Both sites date from the Old
Stone Age. Moreover, some caves and terraces in front of them were excavated:
thus Dr. M. Stekelis on behalf of the Department of Antiquities and the Hebrew
University excavated the Kabbara cave in the south-western Carmel; Misses S.
Barkai and E. Yeivin and Mr. Y. Olamy, under the supervision of Professor Stekelis,
excavated the 'Oren ('Abu Fellaḥ) cave in the 'Oren valley for the Department.
In later seasons the excavations were continued as a joint enterprise of the Department of Antiquities and the Department of Prehistoric Archaeology of the Hebrew
University directed by Professor Stekelis personally. Then again several partial
surface surveys were carried out at Ma'ayan Barukh, Mount Carmel, the Gal'ed
area, the sea-shore at 'Emeq Ḥefer and south of Nethanya, and the neighbourhood
of Zofit. Apart from the above-mentioned workers, pupils of Prof. Stekelis in the
Department of Prehistory at the Hebrew University, and Friends of Antiquities
interested in this aspect of Israel archaeology, took part in the excavations and
study of the finds.
Special importance is to be attached to some new discoveries, which illuminate the
study of prehistory, and shed light on the beginnings of civilization in the Middle
East in general and in Israel in particular. The first and the most important discovery is that of a new Neolithic culture, named the Yarmukian after the locality
in which it was discovered, in the fields of Sha'ar Haggolan. Various remains were
unearthed when fish-ponds were dug in the Mandatory period; later, the exploration of the site was followed by two planned excavations, one on behalf of the
Department of Antiquities and the other on behalf of the IES, both directed by
Professor Stekelis. These remains reveal to us the story of the people of this district
in the New Stone Age, in the early VIth millennium B.C.E. at the latest. These
people of the densely populated triangle formed by the Jordan, the Yarmuk and
the Sea of Galilee, lived by agriculture and, apparently, small cattle breeding. They
engaged also, to a certain extent, in fishing and hunting. They did not yet know the
use of metal, but fashioned a whole series of specialized flint implements for all

their needs. They also knew how to spin and weave, and to make mortars, bowls and other vessels of hard stone. They had, furthermore, a well-developed aesthetic sense, which is evident in their stone, bone and shell jewellery. Some of their cult practices and religious ceremonies are revealed to us not only by their burial customs, but more especially by statuettes and figurines of stone and clay representing steatopygous fertility goddesses with hanging breasts. It can hardly be decided in the light of this evidence whether their society was matriarchal or not.

Some indications of a similar culture were found at Munḥata near Gesher, excavated by Mr. N. Zori.[18]

Of still greater interest were the remains of the transition period, from the use of stone implements alone to the use of stone and metal implements together. It is known as the Chalcolithic (or Aeneolithic) Age. Its remains have been discovered in recent years over almost the whole of Israel, more particularly in four large regions: in the neighbourhood of Beersheba, in Greater Tel Aviv and its vicinity, in the Jordan Valley (Bet-She'an and Kinnereth), and immediately west of the Shefela, the western foothills of the Judaean mountains.

The Beersheba group of settlements is so far the most homogenous and the most intensively investigated. It appears that each one of that group of settlements was inhabited by a separate clan. Its members first found refuge in underground dug-outs hollowed out in the loess soil on the banks of the wadis. These dug-outs were reached from outside by covered passages opening on steep bluffs above the stream-bed, or into vertical pits sunk in the surface of the ground. Some of the dug-outs are connected by subterranean passages. Thus, at Be'er Ẓafad (Bi'r eṣ-Ṣaʿadi) was uncovered a series of six consecutive dug-outs connected by passageways. Bell-shaped silos had been dug in their floors for the storage of food, and some of the dug-outs contained recesses at the sides for household implements. In some dug-outs small, irregular sections of the floor were paved with pebbles painted red with short lines or crossed strokes. The significance of these paved sections is not clear. There are indications that at least some of the dead used to be buried in special niches near the dug-outs, or in disused silos, or under heaped-up stones. Three settlements have so far been examined and studied: Be'er Maṭar, Be'er Ẓafad, and Horvat Beter (Khirbet el-Beyṭar). The first two were excavated by M. Jean Perrot of the *Centre national de la recherche scientifique* of France[19], the last by Dr. I. Ben Dor and subsequently by Dr. M. Dothan for the Department of Antiquities[20]. All three settlements contained traces of four levels of occupation: the lowest two levels were the underground dug-outs; the third contained pits half-sunk underground, continued above ground by rudimentary structures of rubble and pressed

---

[18] See also below, pp. 18 ff.; 40.

[19] For a preliminary report on the excavations at Be'er Maṭar see J. Perrot, IEJ V (1955), pp. 17 ff., 73 ff. Q 167 ff.

[20] M. Dothan, Atiqot II (1959), pp. 1 ff.

mud, and roofed over with wooden beams; the fourth and topmost level consisted of rectangular structures, whose foundations – and these are all that remains – were laid in two or three courses of rubble, limestone or flinty formations. The breaks between one level of settlement and the next were caused by sudden, though not panic-stricken, abandonment of the sites. M. Perrot surmises that these periodic evacuations were caused by years of drought, so common in the Negev, when the inhabitants could not subsist on their dry farming and sought temporary refuge in unaffected areas. Apart from agriculture, the inhabitants lived by livestock breeding and hunting. The bones found include those of domestic cattle, large or small, as well as those of antelopes, various rodents, and small foxes, wild animals that could have been procured only by hunting. In addition to the domestic crafts mentioned earlier in connection with the neolithic culture, evidence of domestic copper metalworking was found, such as small furnaces, crucibles, slag and ore. Metal maceheads, pins, ornaments, and other finished products were also found. Analysis of the metal indicates that it came from the mines of the 'Arava.

At present, it is difficult to find any appreciable differences between the cultures represented by the four strata of occupation; it seems that all of them belonged to a more or less uniform stage. The pottery is of especial interest. On the one hand it is related to types already known from the excavations at Tuleylat Ghassul, in the Plains of Moab north of the Dead Sea. On the other hand new types of different painted and plastic decorations are relatively abundant. A unique vessel, dubbed „churn", as it fully resembles the leather container used even now by the Bedawin to produce their semi-liquid butter, appears in comparatively large numbers[21]). In contradistinction to Neolithic pottery, the use of a *tournette* is evident here, the rims of most of the vessels having been turned. The impressions of the mats used as *tournettes* are visible on the flat bottoms of many vessels, and some vases bear the distinctive mark of the string used to cut the pot off the wheel. There was a considerable improvement in the art of making basalt bowls, many of which were decorated with incised bands of geometric patterns. Most of the bowls were discovered in sets of three, two deeper ones with flat bases and a shallower one with a flattened base resting on a tripod whose three legs are connected by a circular band at the foot (pl. I, 3). Stone, bone and occasional metal ornaments are common. Several bone figurines (pl. I, 2), which served as amulets or representations of gods, were also found. M. Perrot, who conducted the excavations at two of these settlements, is of the opinion that each settlement was made up of groups specializing in a single craft. Be'er Matar, e.g., specialized in metalwork.

Remains of similar cultures have been found within the area of Greater Tel Aviv,

---

[21]) Similar, though smaller, so-called bird vases, were found in small number also at Tuleylat Ghasul. About the bird-vases and churns see R. Amiran, BASOR 130 (1953), pp. 11 ff.; J. Kaplan, BIES XVIII (1954), pp. 64 ff.

and excavated and examined jointly by the Department of Antiquities and the Municipality of Tel Aviv. Excavations were financed by the Municipality and directed by Dr. J. Kaplan. Similar remains were found at Bene Beraq, which were excavated by Dr. Kaplan on behalf of the Department of Antiquities. Graves here of this period contained a considerable number of friable and broken clay ossuaries similar to those found at Ḥadera during the thirties. These indicate that the collection of bones was customary at the time. In later periods the custom died out, and no trace of it is found in actual remains, in figurative representations, or in documents, from the third millennium to the Ist century B.C.E. A small ossuary which may have served as a toy is of special interest. Among the vessels placed in the graves as funerary offerings, particular mention should be made of small clay bowls or tripods, similar to the Chalcolithic stone bowls from the neighbourhood of Beersheba (pl. I, 3). It has hitherto been thought that these clay vessels were used for burning incense, but in the light of the finds at Beersheba, it seems likely that these were cheap imitations of the stone vases too valuable to be buried with the dead (?).

Chalcolithic cemeteries have been discovered also at other places in the vicinity of Tel Aviv. At 'Azor, work in a quarry revealed the presence of a spacious burial cave, which collapsed anciently squashing a large number of pottery ossuaries. M. Jean Perrot, of the *Centre national de la recherche scientifique*, kindly undertook to direct this excavation on behalf of the Department of Antiquities. It became obvious at once that the pottery ossuaries in this cave represented a series of entirely new types, and the subsequent painstaking reconstruction of the crushed sherds, undertaken with much care and limitless patience by Mrs. J. Hillmann-Schacherl, the formatore of the Department, brought to light an endless variety of these receptacles, the overwhelming majority rectangular (pl. II, 1), some on short feet, as if imitating houses erected on piles, with curving, vaulted roofs and high protrusions over the entrance (in the short façade) and the opposite backwall, while a few were round. One rather suggests the shape of a sheep. Several have applied decorations suggesting protruding ends of wooden beams; many are painted. Practically all show a very prominent curved nose stuck onto the elevated protrusion over the entrance, while one exhibits on the same protrusion also other features of the human face painted in purple. Highly decayed human bones were found both inside and outside the ossuaries, as well as numerous objects laid in the cave as funerary equipment.

A small group of tombs of the same period at Giv'ataim, recently investigated on behalf of the Department by Misses S. Barkai and V. Zwilichovsky, produced also shallow rectangular undressed stone ossuaries with flat flagstone covers. The same cemetery that continued in use during the first two phases of the EC period produced another surprise in the form of a narrow bladed bronze dagger considerably thickened down the middle, obviously cast in a closed mould.

Chalcolithic remains have been found near the Tell of Rosh Ha'ayin by Dr. J. Kaplan for the IES,[22] and at the foot of the Tell of Lod (Lydda) excavated by Dr. J. Kaplan for the Department of Antiquities. They were also found in two small mounds near Tel Battish in the valley of Soreq (near Bet-Shemesh), which were excavated by Dr. Kaplan for the IES.[23]

Remains of an extensive Chalcolithic – EC settlement area were also revealed at the so-called Tel Gat (Tell Sheykh el-'Areyni). Here the Department of Antiquities has been conducting a large scale investigation during the last three years under the direction of S. Yeivin (and in his absence, of S. Levy), both in the *tell* itself as well as in the high terrace surrounding the elevated mound on three sides[24]. On the SE edge of that terrace were found so-far remains of eleven strata without reaching yet virgin soil. The uppermost layer (I) definitely proves that the settlement came to an end during the second phase of the EC period (about the middle of the IIIrd millennium B.C.E.). Strata II – III date to EC II and I. Stratum IV seems to be transitional from Chalcolithic to the EC times, and possibly also some of the under-lying strata (V – VI?). Lower levels (strata VII – XI) apparently represent purely Chalcolithic cultures. The bearers of that culture were sedentary agriculturers who mastered the builders' craft to the extent of erecting large buildings with thick walls constructed of shaped rectangular mud-bricks laid in straight courses well bounded together, some of them still standing to a height of 3 m. They grew wheat and flax, and cultivated olives, from which they extracted oil. They practiced spin-ning and weaving, threw pots on wheels, and were fairly skilled in metallurgy.

The pottery of this settlement shows distinct connections both with the Ghas-sulian culture, which may represent the peripheral settlements of the south-eastern Jordan Valley, northern Negev and Transjordan[25]), on the one hand, and that of Megiddo and Bet-She'an, on the other. It is to be hoped that the continued ex-cavation of this site may clarify the origin and connections of the various stages of Chalcolithic cultures in the country.

The main problem araising in connection with this settlement is the source of its water supply, since no flowing springs are present now in the vicinity. The only possibility seems to be the use of shallow wells dug as need arose in the dry beds of the creeks north and south of the tell, on the assumption that the underground water table was anciently higher than at present.

That problems connected with the storage of water loomed large in settlements of this period is proved by the excavation of another Chalcolithic site in a springless area in the central Sharon, at Mezer. Two seasons of excavations directed by M.

---

[22]) A preliminary report by J. Kaplan, IEJ VIII (1958), pp. 149 ff.

[23]) A preliminary report by J. Kaplan, BIES XIX (1955), pp. 245 ff.

[24]) See below, pp. 29–31; a preliminary report on this excavation, S. Yeivin, *Excavations at Tel "Gat" Preliminary Report on the first three seasons, 1956–1958*, Jerusalem, 1960.

[25]) According to recently announced investigations in the vicinity of Petra.

Dothan have revealed here three layers of occupation belonging to the Ghassulian and Late Chalcolithic stages, to be dated probably to the XXXIVth – XXXIIIrd centuries B.C.E. A so-far unique feature were two rock cut cisterns which were used for the storage of water, though excavated in the lime-stone rock and not plastered at all.[26])

A cemetery of the Ghassulian period investigated by Mr. M. Prausnitz at Kabri in western Galilee produced a number of remarkably well finished stone vessels (pl. II, 2), and dated a large core of obsidian previously discovered (with some of the vessels) on the spot[27]), proving the existence of an import-export commerce in raw materials, and accidentally confirming the role of Canaan as an intermediary in the obsidian trade between Armenia and Egypt at such an early date.

Mr. M. Prausnitz also examined during two short seasons a low *tell* known as Tel 'Ely (Kh. Sheykh 'Aly) in the Jordan Valley. Under a disturbed and largely destroy-ed layer of the Byzantine – Early Arab period, a Chalcolithic settlement has been discovered. The structural remains closely resemble the topmost layer of Tuleylat Ghassul, while the pottery resembles both the Ghassulian culture and the cultures from the Beersheba district. Below the Chalcolithic layer there was a Neolithic level of occupation (stratum III) with stone foundations of parallel rectangular rooms, each about 15 m. long, built inside a large enclosed courtyard open to the sky. A comparatively large number of sherds of open bowls exhibited a peculiar decoration of parallel incisions in long wavy lines both on the inside and outside surfaces of the vessel. Stratum IV represents a pre-pottery Neolithic level with stone foundations of buildings, and three headless contracted burials under the beaten earth floors. Signs of denudation in this layer show that there was some lapse of time between the end of this settlement and the reoccupation of the site in Chal-colithic times.

Recent excavations supply us, therefore, with an almost uninterrupted series of cultures from the Late Mesolithic to the EC I Ages. The latest link in this chain (at least in the northern and central parts of the country), the transition from the Esdraelon culture to EC I period has been made clear by the excavation of the mass grave near Tell el-'Asawir.

Here was investigated, by Dr. M. Dothan, a large burial cave, the top of which was occupied with numerous typical Hyksos inhumations. Under these was a sterile filling of earth some 0.5 m thick, below which over the bottom of the cave were spread numerous dismembered burials accompanied by funerary offerings, in-cluding numerous pottery vessels, semi-precious stone and shell beads, and some pendants. These ceramic products included vessels of Late Chalcolithic types,

---

[26]) Preliminary notice and reports in RB LXV (1958), pp. 414–6; M. Dothan, IEJ VII (1957), pp. 217 ff.; IX (1959), pp. 13 ff.
[27]) M. Stekelis, EI V (1958), pp. 35 ff.

among them burnished bowls of the Esdraelon culture, as well as typical painted pots of the EC I phase, thus providing the connecting link between the Chalcolithic and Canaanite (Bronze) Ages.

Apart from the problem of relative chronology – the placing of one culture in relation to another – there remains the problem of absolute chronology – the establishing of the period of time when the entire complex of those cultures existed within the chronological framework of the Ancient East as a whole. This problem again is bound up with another. Where was the cradle of man's cultural development in this centre of world history? The two earliest cultural foci, the Late Predynastic and Sumerian cultures of Egypt and Mesopotamia respectively, appear to us relatively well-developed, and their connection with what preceded them in the Valleys of the Nile or the Tigris and Euphrates is obscure. These cultures, moreover, were based on an advanced stage of development in the use of irrigation in agriculture. They knew how to control flood waters and how to make use of local hydrographic conditions. They had also a thorough knowledge of metal working. Control of flood waters can be effective only in a well-knit society with a fairly well-developed culture. When one remembers this, and since wild species of cereals are unknown both in Egypt and in Mesopotamia, it is difficult to conceive that these countries were the cradle of agriculture. Without agriculture civilization cannot arise. In addition, these countries lack deposits of copper ore.

The western part of the Fertile Crescent – the countries of the eastern Mediterranean littoral, Israel, Lebanon, and Syria – is the chief habitat of wild cereals. Here there obtained optimal conditions both for irrigation farming near numerous small springs requiring no control of flood waters (and thus no pre-existing well-knit social organization), and dry farming, at first in the beds of creeks that dry up in the summer, and later in more extensive areas. In this belt deposits of copper are found at its two extremes: in the Armenian massif on the north, which is difficult of access, and in the 'Arava south of the Dead Sea, in shallow deposits easily reached by land routes.

In this connection the results of excavations at Jericho, in the Jordanian area of the old Land of Israel, in recent years merit serious consideration. Here were found remains of several fortification-walls, surrounding superimposed strata of Neolithic settlements all belonging to the period of the dawn of man's cultural achievement, which preceded the use of pottery. It is open to discussion whether the establishment of a settlement can be taken as evidence of a definite social organization, but it is indisputable that fortifications requiring a concerted effort can only be built if there is a centralized social organization. It is, therefore, quite plausible to suggest now that the Land of Israel was the cradle of man's cultural development in his first advance beyond the end of the Middle Stone Age to the Chalcolithic Age. It is possible for the student to study here the Mesolithic Age, with its first fumbling experiments with wild cereals not deliberately sown, the earliest aesthetic expression in bone and stone, and the possible birth of religious concepts.[28] The student can further watch here the Middle Stone Age merging into the Neo-lithic or New Stone Age. He can observe the remains of conscious agricultural activity and the social organization implicit in the early fortifications at Jericho. In the New Stone Age artistic forms and religious cults developed, leaving behind them the evidence of the skulls from Jericho, whose facial features have been moulded in plaster, the clay figurines from Jericho XI and stone figurines of the Yarmukian culture of Sha'ar Haggolan and Tel Aviv, and painted pottery. Finally, in the Chalcolithic Age agriculture was relatively advanced and there was model-ling and sculpture in clay, bone and stone. Man was then able to engage in a metal industry, painted ornamentation on pottery and the realistic paintings on the walls of buildings at Tuleylat Ghassul. Painted clay ossuaries provide not only evidence of burial customs, but show the great variety of architectural forms current (pl. II, 1). If this is so, it follows that the impulses to cultural development, both technical and spiritual, came from here; and when they reached countries whose hydrographic and climatic conditions were more favourable and made intensive agriculture pos-sible, they accelerated the development of rich and highly-advanced civilizations, which quickly eclipsed and obscured the rate of development in the modest centre on the Mediterranean littoral[29].

When considering the connection with earlier periods, importance should be attached to a small excavation on the terrace in front of the 'Oren cave in the 'Oren creek in Western Carmel. Several stone circles were discovered in the topmost level. They seems to have been the foundations of tents or light booths built of twigs and rushes; with these were associated flint implements of the Tahu-nian phase of Neolithic cultures. The complete stratification of the terrace has not yet been determined, but a section through the debris forming the terrace, revealed while a road was built nearby, shows layers belonging to the Middle Stone Age. The layers hold remains of human burials of that period. The excavations will be continued, and it is possible that here will be found the evidence for linking these successive cultures of the Middle and Late Stone Ages up to the Tahunian. Lately the presence of Mesolithic remains under the Neolithic strata has been reported from Jericho.

## V.  *Excavations: Canaanite Remains*

Proceeding to review now the new material concerning the various periods of the Canaanite (Bronze) Age civilizations, it is expedient to start with the exploration

---

[28] Cf. J. Perrot, Antiquity and Survival II/2–3 (1957), pp. 1 ff.
[29] S. Yeivin, ibid., pp. 111 ff.

of Bet-Yeraḥ (Kh. Kerak), for through its lowest, Chalcolithic, stratum it ties-in well with the preceding survey.

Tel Bet-Yeraḥ is the largest *tell* in Israel as far as area is concerned. When the Arthur Ruppin Agricultural School was about to be built on the southern side of the *tell* in the mid-1940s, and later the „Oholo" buildings in memory of the late Berl Katznelson on the northern side were to be erected, the Mandatory Department of Antiquities insisted on carrying out soundings on both sites, in order to examine the stratification and possible finds. The IES agreed to do the work. It was accomplished under the direction of Dr. B. Mazar and M. Stekelis in the spring of 1944 on the southern site, and of Mr. M. Avi-Yonah and M. Stekelis during 1945/6 on the northern[30]). A considerable part of the buildings on both sites had already been erected before the establishment of the State. The Government of Israel was requested in 1949 to permit some expansion on these institutions. Under the circumstances, it had been impossible to refuse a request so vital to the builders; however, it was insisted upon that there should be an archaeological investigation of the additional areas before building was begun, with the stipulation that further construction would only be allowed if no structures requiring preservation for historical or archaeological reasons were to be uncovered in such areas. In this way, the Israel Department of Antiquities began in 1950 excavations in two areas, and continued digging through several extended seasons. At first they were under the direction of the late P.L.O. Guy; then, since 1951, under the direction of his assistant, Mr. P. Bar-Adon.

In the southern part of the *tell*, at the highest point, a sounding was made (10 × 10 m) down to virgin soil in the steep accumulation overhanging Lake Gennezareth. The remains of sixteen strata were found, some of them exhibiting a number of stages, twenty-four stages in all. From this dig and from the subsequent excavation to the south and west of this pit, it became clear that settlement at this place began at the end of the Chalcolithic period and continued uninterrupted until the First Phase of the Middle Canaanite (Bronze) period in the first quarter of the second millennium B.C.E. Some graves belonging to the Second Phase of the MC were also uncovered here. Then the site was abandoned, and remained so intil the LI period (Persian Domination) in the IVth (?) century B.C.E. Since then the place was occupied until the middle of the Early Arab period in the VIIIth–IXth centuries C.E.

The clear evidence of a rich and closely-knit society provided the archaeologists with their greatest surprise. This society fortified the place, stored grain on a large scale, and in the middle of the third millennium B.C.E. laid out straight streets and paved them with basalt (pl. II, 3). Remains of a large military camp were found in the Roman layer. An additional discovery along the entire southern and a con-

---

[30]) Maisler, Stekelis & Avi-Yonah, IEJ II (1952), pp. 165 ff., 218 ff.

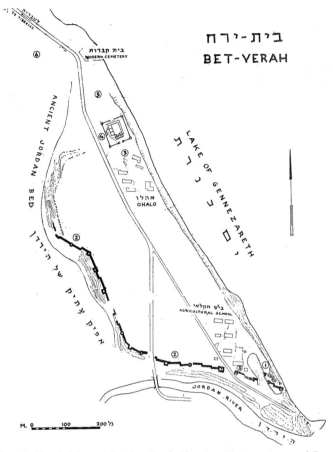

בית-ירח

BET-YERAH

Fig. 5. Sketch-Map of Tel Bet-Yerah Showing Various Areas of Excavations and the Hellenistic
Fortifications.

1. Excavations of the Department of Antiquities.
2. Hellenistic Fortifications.
   Excavations of the Department of Antiquities.
3. Excavations of the Israel Exploration Society.
4. Synagogue Enclosure.
   Excavations of the Department of Antiquities.
5. Area of the Excavations of the Oriental Institute, Chicago
   University.
6. Remains of Roman Bridge.

siderable part of the western edge of the *tell* was a series of fortifications belonging to different stages of the Early Canaanite period. A huge stone substructure, 4–7 m. wide and 3–4 m. high, for a mudbrick wall of the Hellenistic period, was also uncovered (fig. 5). It was fortified with alternate square and circular or semi-circular towers at regular intervals. This system of fortifications was at first wrongly attributed to the First Phase of the MC period. To it belong the remains of a southern re-entrant gateway between two very strong towers, and a narrow, and possibly secret postern lined with limestone slabs[31]).

An interesting excavation was also made at Rosh Hanniqra (Khirbet eṭ-Ṭaba'iq), which sheds new light on EC fortifications and has helped to clarify a number of obscure points in connection with the fortifications of 'Ay. The excavation was directed at first by Mrs. R. Amiran, and later by Mrs. M. Tadmor and Mr. M. Prausnitz.[32])

Messrs. P. Bar-Adon and B. Ravani directed a sounding in the western part of ancient Tiberias in connection with the erection of a plant for the purification of sewage. Here were examined remains of a settlement, belonging to the EC period. After a gap of thousands of years, strata dated to the Early Roman – Byzantine – Arab periods had been superimposed on the Canaanite remains.

Another small sounding at the foot of Tel Raqqat, north of Tiberias, made in connection with the widening of the highway, revealed that this edge of the hill, on top of which rises the *tell* proper, was inhabited during the EC II – IV times, and then abandoned. Above the three EC strata were remains of an EI I (XIIth – XIth century B.C.E.) occupation, which could not be connected with any definite building remains[33]).

The most interesting excavation dealing with Canaanite remains was that conducted by M. Dothan on the sea-shore at Nehariyya in Galilee. Here remains of a MC temple were investigated by Dr. I. Ben-Dor on behalf of the Mandatory Department of Antiquities in 1947[34]). Subsequent accidental finds in the immediate vicinity of these remains confirmed the presence of further ancient remains in the area. Three seasons of excavations proved that this sacred area, apparently connected with a sweet water spring which is now just below the water mark of the sea, owing to the gradual sinking of the coast line, was first founded in the Hyksos period (MC II). It comprised then a modest square cella (erected on stone foundations) with a small round high-place heaped up of rubble, on which the devotees of the deity could deposit their votive offerings, consisting of bronze, silver and gold jewellery, semi-precious stone beads, silver strips with lightly chased images of the

---

[31]) A full report on this excavation is now in an advanced stage of preparation.
[32]) Miriam Tadmor and M. Prausnitz, 'Atiqot II (1959), pp. 72 ff.; M. Prausnitz, 'Atiqot I (1955), p. 139.
[33]) Cf. below, p. 26 (excavations at Gat and Hazor resp.).
[34]) I. Ben-Dor, QDAP XIV (1950), pp. 1 ff.

goddess worshipped at this shrine, pottery figurines of animals and birds, small models of various pots and – mostly – bowls containing each seven tumblers most probably used as libation vessels, for they were mostly found surrounded by patches of oily matter. Later, a large rectangular temple was erected NW of the original chapel, while over the latter was heaped up a larger high place with a flight of steps leading up to its center (from the west); the former small „bama" was abandoned. The whole area was apparently enclosed, for remains of a square pillar forming the eastern jamb of the doorway were uncovered south of the latter temple, in alignment with its entrance, and partly overlying the former high-place. This new courtyard contained also remains of a built stone altar. Still later the temple building was enlarged by the addition of rooms both to the east and west of the original area. The whole was destroyed, and the site abandoned, sometime in the XVIth century B.C.E. during one of the Egyptian raids under the early XVIIIth Dynasty.

One of the most interesting finds in this area was half of a mould, in which were cast statuettes of the goddess to whom the temple must have been dedicated, probably the "'atrat yam" celebrated in the Ugaritic epic texts (pl. III, 1)[34]a).

In 1955 Dr. Y. Yadin, of the Hebrew University, assisted by an able staff of experienced Israeli archaeologists, began a systematic four seasons exploration of the site of Hazor on behalf of the J. de Rothschild's Expedition. All in all ten areas were investigated, three on the high mound and seven within the confines of the much larger but also much lower „enclosure" (fig. 6). As a result one may state that the history of this settlement, first identified as ancient Hazor by the late J. Garstang[35]), begins about the mid-EC period and ends in early Hellenistic times, with certain gaps of occupation.

The most interesting revelation, however, was the fact that the so-called „enclosure" was not merely a stabling camp for chariotry, as suggested by some scholars, but a densely populated and well fortified city, founded in the early Hyksos days (MC II a) and continuosly inhabited till the end of the LC period, showing four superimposed strata of occupation (the lower two MC, and upper two LC) wherever tested throughout its length and width (ares C, D, E, F, H, K, and 210). In one spot, over the ruined walls of the latest LB city near the gate, there were remains of a poor and obviously short-lived last occupation after the destruction of the fortified city, sometimes during the late XIIIth century B.C.E.

In the LC city were uncovered three sacred areas. Area H contained a large building consisting of an inner courtyard, an open pro-naos with two columns flanking the entrance to the naos, and an inner cella with a square niche in its northern wall on the main axis of the building. The inner faces of the wall were lined with a row of smooth slabs of basalt at a slight height above floor level. The furnishing of the

---

[34]a) M. Dothan, IEJ VI (1956), pp. 14 ff.      [35]) J. Garstang, AAA XIV (1927), pp. 35 ff.

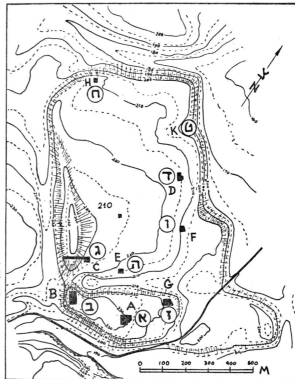

Fig. 6.
Sketch-map of Hazor (tell and enclosure) showing the Various Excavated Areas. (By kindness of Dr. Y. Yadin, Director of the James de Rotschilds' Expedition).

Fig. 9.
Plan of Stratum X (XIth-Xth centuries B.C.E.) at el-Khirbe (Qasile) showing Two Rows of "Four-Spaced" Buildings. (By Kindness of Dr. B. Mazar, Director of the IES's Expedition).

room included among other things a basalt altar decorated with the symbol of the sun, a large decorated basalt cauldron (for libations?), and some large pottery *pithoi*. Further investigations revealed that the temple was first erected in the MC period, and shows four phases of rebuilding corresponding to the four strata found throughout the enclosure. In the early LC phase the entrance to the pro-naos was flanked by a basalt orthostat bearing a life size lion in relief with its forequarters cut in the round (pl. III, 2)[36].

A second sacred area, with a large open courtyard in the middle of which stood a large monolithic altar was uncovered in Area F, in the eastern part of the „enclosure", connected with a series of long subterranean tunnels, the purpose and final destination of which could not be clarified. These were later partly used as burial caves, and yielded rich funerary equipment[37].

The third sacred area was a modest temple in the latest LC stratum near the fortification rempart in the SW part of the enclosure. In a niche were found a statuette of a seated god, a series of small anepigraphic basalt stelae, on one of which were sculptured in relief two arms uplifted to a sun-and-crescent symbol, a small orthostat with the relief of a lion, and a seated basalt statuette of a god (?). Among other finds there was also a small bronze standard of a snake goddess covered with silver foil.[38].

Investigations on the *tell* proper showed that in the LC period it was a prosperous settlement with a large public building (palace?) in Area A, in the center of the mound, the entrance of which up a stone built staircase had probably been flanked by basalt orthostats, of which only a head of a lioness in the round was found; again the entrance to the building proper from the inner courtyard was paved and lined in basalt, with a large tapering anepigraphic basalt stele near it. This city was violently destroyed and abandoned[39].

Epigraphic material of the LC period at Hazor included a baked-pottery model of a liver inscribed in cuneiform and a small fragment of a granite stele showing bits of three columns of a hieroglyphic inscription of the XIXth dynasty.[40].

The municipality of Tel Aviv-Jaffa in cooperation with the Department of Antiquities sponsors an archaeological expedition conducted by Dr. J. Kaplan, the Municipal archaeologist, in the ancient *tell* of Jaffa. During the three campaigns (1955, 1956, 1958) an area of some 800 sq. m. was investigated, which proved to cover the NE angle of the ancient settlement. The lowest layer reached so far was a glacis, and a thick mud-brick wall of Hyksos times, through which was cut a gateway in the early reign of Ramses II (1290–1234 B.C.E.). Fragments of sandstone

[36]) Y. Yadin, IEJ VIII (1958), pp. 11 ff.
[37]) Ibid., pp. 9 ff.
[38]) Y. Yadin et alii, *The Hazor Excavations* I, Jerusalem, 1958.
[39]) Y. Yadin, BIES XXIII (1959), pp. 17 ff.
[40]) Ibid., p. 21.

doorjambs inscribed with the cartouches of that pharaoh were found partly here
and partly reused in the higher stratum (pl. III, 3). A comparatively wide, straight
and stone-paved street, between two rows of mud-brick houses, led WSW into
the city. This settlement was destroyed in an extensive conflagration, apparently
when Merenptah recaptured the city following disturbances in Canaan in his third
year. He rebuilt it on the same plan, with a large gateway directly over that of his
father, with a heavy stone threshold, on which were found *in-situ* a central upright
stone, on which closed the two leaves of the gate, and a heavy bronze shoe into
which was originally fitted the lower pivot of the southern wooden leaf of the gate.
This layer of occupation was again destroyed by fire probably during the invasion
of the sea-peoples[41]).

No other excavation during the period under review brought to light strata of the
period, apart from cemeteries or individual graves at Gesher Hazziv and Hanita (in
western Galilee), and Kefar Ruppin (in the valley of Bet-She'an), the former excavated on behalf of the Department by Dr. Z. Goldman, the latter by Mr. N.
Zori[42]).

## VI.  *Excavations: Israelite Remains*

Numerous large and small scale excavations have revealed remains of EI period,
apart from the burials dealt with above[43]).

New light on the early Israelite settlement in Canaan was shed by several excavations. On the *tell* proper of Hazor, above the ruins of the LC city was found a layer,
in which appeared small patches of pebble or stone pavements that were not connected with any building remains. The pottery associated with these scattered remains could be dated to the XIIth century B.C.E. and was of the rough village type
connected with the early Israelite settlements elsewhere in Galilee[44]). Hence this
layer was assigned by the excavators to early Israelite semi-nomadic squatters.

Since similar small paved patches of the same period were uncovered on the high
terrace round the acropolis hill of the so-called Tel „Gat"[45]), and pottery of the
same period without any apparent building remains connected with it was also
found over the EC remains at the edge of Tel Raqqat (about 3 km north of Tiberias)[46]), it is obvious that such squatting of early Israelite settlers in the late

---

[41]) The author is indebted to Dr. Y. J. Kaplan for the details of this exploration and for his kind
permission to include them here before the publication of his report.
[42]) On the LC cemetery at Tell Abu Hawam see above, p. 11.
[43]) See above, pp. 11–12.
[44]) Y. Aharoni, EI IV (1956), pp. 56 ff.
[45]) See above, pp. 22.
[46]) See above, p. 22.

XIIIth – early XIIth century B.C.E. was a common feature throughout the country. However, no arable land was available in Galilee for these new aspirants to agriculture within the densely settled Canaanite area, so that they had to carve for themselves new agricultural areas out of the wooded parts of central Galilee. An investigation of such a settlement was made by Dr. Y. Aharoni on behalf of the Department of Antiquities at Tel Harashim (Kh. et-Tuleyl) in the high mountainous central Galilee. There, two Israelite strata were laid bare. The earliest (Stratum III), founded on virgin rock, dates to the end of the XIIIth – beginning of the XIIth century B.C.E. and reflects still semi-nomadic occupations, since its main feature was a small workshop for smelting and casting metal[47]. It was here that the typical rough (village-) style pottery of the period has been properly dated and fitted into its place. After an occupational gap the place was resettled early in the MI period, and Stratum II showed remains of a small fortress with casemate walls. Stratum I (entirely denuded) was represented only by a comparative abundance of LI (Persian) and Hellenistic sherds[48].

The MI period was well represented in the excavations of Tel Hazor. The first Israelite urban settlement (Stratum X) dates to the reign of Solomon (appr. 970–930 B.C.E.), as reported in the Bible[49]. It occupied the western half of the high mound and was surrounded by a casemate wall, pierced on the east by a fortified gateway, identical in plan and construction with the northern gate of Megiddo (Stratum IV)[50]. The eastern part of the wall defending the most vulnerable side of the city was strengthened by a glacis and protected by a deep moat in front of the latter.

Under Ahab the Israelite city was extended eastwards to include the whole area of the high mound, and a new system of fortifications erected around it, with the large citadel at the W. end of the city. Investigations here were conducted by Mrs. Ruth Amiran (at the W. end) and Mrs. Trude Dothan (at the E. end)[51].

The settled area in and around Hazor is not limited to the *tell* proper and the large MC and LC enclosure; a whole series of „suburbs" extends eastwards along the northern bluff overhanging the Hazor creek, mostly buried now under the modern settlement of Ayyelet Hashshahar. Levelling operations undertaken by this settle-

---

[47] For a typical group of semi-nomads engaged among other things also in metallurgy see S. Yeivin, Atiqot II (1959), pp. 155 ff. Even nowdays the semi-nomadic Nawar and Sleyb in the ME are both small cattle breeders on a small scale and itinerant black-smiths; so were the east-Euroepan gypsies till a short time ago.

[48] See above, note 44.

[49] I *Kings* 9 : 15.

[50] Yadin, has already proved that an identical gateway at Gezer, hitherto wrongly attributed to the Hasmonean period, belongs also to Solomonic times (IEJ VIII (1958), pp. 80 ff.). Cf. the above mentioned biblical quotation (note 49), which mentions only these three cities: Hazor, Megiddo and Gezer.

[51] Y. Yadin, IEJ VIII (1958), pp. 4 ff.

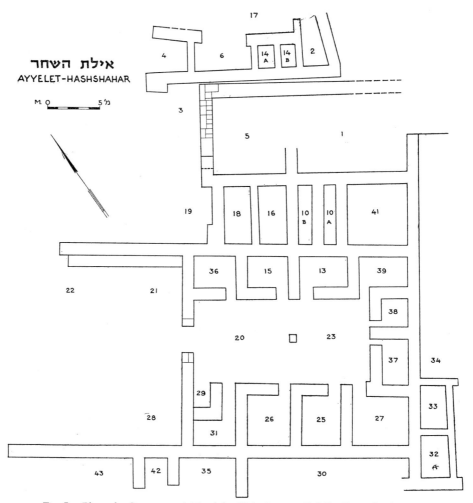

Fig. 7.   Plan of a Caravanserai (?) of the IXth Century B.C.E., East of Tel Hazor.

ment in 1950 in order to enlarge their collective dining-hall, uncovered two deep drains lined with hard baked pottery rings. The late P.L.O. Guy with the assistance of M. Dothan investigated these remains on behalf of the Department, and found the remains of a large LI (Persian) residence built of thick *terre pisée* walls interspersed with thin layers of lime-plaster. The drains were in the middle of a large central courtyard. A large amount of MC sherds testifies to an occupation dating to that period, the building remains of which were entirely destroyed by the LI builders, if they ever existed.

In the winter of 1955/6 the same *qevuẓa* used a bulldozer to level off another area at the eastern end of their settlement, in order to erect a new pen-house for their sheep. In the course of operations they struck a corner of a wall built of limestone ashlar. The Department of Antiquities was called in to investigate. A limited excavation, directed by S. Yeivin, revealed the presence of structural remains belonging to two superimposed strata. The upper one, dating to the LI and early Hellenistic times was almost entirely destroyed in the course of levelling operations (with the exception of one square room). Immediately under this were uncovered the stone foundations (pebbles and small boulders of basalt, no quarried stone at all) of a large caravanserai of the IXth century B.C.E. (fig. 7), and part of an adjacent building of seemingly similar dimension and purpose. Here again there were in the debris comparatively large numbers of MC sherds, as well as fragmentary EI pots of the above mentioned rough village type[52]).

The presence of this series of large commercial (?) buildings outside the city proper, but apparently within a fortified enclosure[53]), suggests the possibility of assigning this suburb to an extraterritorial foreign merchant colony, such as is apparently hinted at in the Bible under the term of „streets" (          )[54]).

Again, the Department's excavations at Tel „Gat" (Tell el-'Areyni)[55]) revealed a number of MI strata (IV – VI) on the acropolis hill. The topmost (IV) was destroyed during the Babylonian invasion. Its fortifications, which closely follow the configuration on top of the hill, have entirely disappeared, since their remains had been weathered away and swept down the slopes during the period of abandonment of the site in the VIth century B.C.E. In stratum V the acropolis was defended on its NW corner by a great square (?) tower, a large part of which has also dis-

---

[52]) See above, p. 27. Here, again it is possible that this pottery may point to the presence of semi-nomadic squatters, who did not erect any permanent buildings. Would it be feasible to assign the MC pottery to similar squatting during the Age of the Patriarchs?

[53]) There were indications of a thick fortification wall north of the uncovered buildings, which, unfortunately, could not be investigated.

[54]) I *Kings* 21 : 34. The Hebrew *ḥuṣot* though used for streets, literally means *outsides*, which may very well refer to suburbs *outside* the city wall, just as well as to open spaces for circulation outside the houses (= streets).

[55]) See above, p. 16.

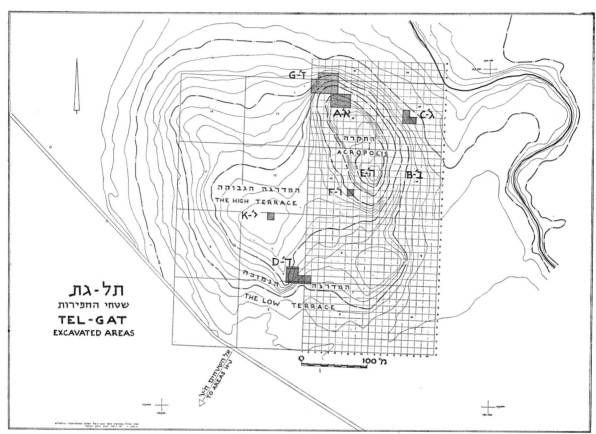

Fig. 8.   Sketch-map of the So-called Tel "Gat", Showing the Various Excavated Areas.

appeared with the subsequent denudation on the edge of the *tell*, all the more easily gone since its western part had been erected over an artificial „fill". This stratum, too, seems to belong to the VIIth century B.C.E. Stratum VIII apparently dates to the IXth century B.C.E. It was defended by a casemate wall. The front-wall of the casemates disappeared long ago with the remains of the later strata, but a short stretch of the hind-wall, and stumps of the side partitions, of the casemates were revealed on the slope of the acropolis. The early decision of the expedition to start digging at this part of the acropolis, so as to uncover the gateway of the fortifications, was fully justified, this stretch of the hind-wall showed remains of several casemates. In five of them entrances could be located. Four of these were comparatively narrow, sited in pairs in adjacent corners of the casemates, while the middle casemate was twice as wide as the others, and its wide entrance was situated in the middle of the hind-wall. Moreover, a buttressing narrow wall at the back (inside the city) was interrupted at this doorway, while the area in front of it, inside the city, was paved with small flag-stones (pl. IV, 1). Obviously, here was the city gate with a paved square in front of it (fig. 8). Below this casemate wall there are remains of two other casemated fortification systems immediately over-lying remains of a burnt-brick city-walls with a wide gateway, apparently belong-ing to a Canaanite level of occupation[56] (fig. 8, 6).

The excavations of Jaffa[57] have revealed the presence of MI levels unfortunately badly ruined by the deep foundations of modern buildings, but a fair amount of interesting pottery was gleaned here.

With the support of the Tel Aviv municipality, the IES has for three seasons carried out excavations at el-Khirbe (in the lands of Qasile), on the northern bank of the Yarkon river, under the direction of Professor B. Mazar. Here were revealed the remains of a city which was inhabited, with short intervals, from the XIIth century B.C.E. to the XIIIth–XIVth century C.E. Twelve levels of occupation were uncovered, the first Philistine, the last Mameluk. In Stratum X (the third above virgin soil) the place was a considerable centre of industry, engaged in metallurgy, in dyeing textiles, and possibly in weaving. In the excavated section of the mound two sets of houses of identical plan – the type of rectangular four-roomed buildings – were uncovered at this level, one at each side of a straight street (fig. 9)[57a]. A large inn was also found at this level, that undoubtedly served the traders who came in caravans or ships. During the Israelite period (layers IX–VII, from the conquest of the town by David until its destruction by Tiglath-Pileser III) the place was a flourishing port surrounded by a casemate wall. A large government building stood there, and the two Hebrew ostraca found on the surface of the *tell*, some years before the excavations began, probably originate from it. The collection of Israelite

---

[56]  S. Yeivin, *The Excavations of Tel "Gat"*, Jerusalem, 1960.

[57]  See above, pp. 25–26 and note 41.

[57a]  See above, p. 24.

pottery unearthed in these levels is also interesting, in particular a large jar decorated with a figure of a horse reserved in a creamy slip (?), while the rest of the surface was covered with a burnished reddish-brown slip. In many courtyards of the
Israelite level were found small heaps of clay sinkers (from nets or looms) heaped
with ash; large bowls were usually placed on top of these heaps. It is clear that these
served to keep the food in the bowls hot. In the author's opinion, they were
primitive types of *chalant* arrangements for the Shabbat, when the kindling of fire
was forbidden by Mosaic law[58]).

At Khirbet Saleh, a low but typical *tell* near Ramat Rahel, comparatively extensive
excavations were carried out in 1954 and 1955. They were directed by Dr. Y. Aharoni, on behalf of the Department of Antiquities and the IES. In the north-eastern
corner of the *tell* a large Byzantine church was discovered, its mosaic floors decorated with geometrical designs, and with a complex of monastic buildings attached
to it. This complex is most probably to be identified with the Kathisma Church
mentioned in contemporary sources. At the centre of the *tell* were found the remains of a Byzantine level, including some fortifications; under these were buildings dated to the period of the Return from the Exile. Beneath these, again, were
remains of a casemate wall from the period of the kings of Judah (IXth–VIIIth centuries B.C.E.). The finds include two proto-Aeolic capitals[59]) and a fragment of a
third from the Israelite fortress, as well as a large number of seal impressions from
the days of the First and Second Temple (*lammelekh, Zif; Yhd; Yrwšlm*; private
seal impressions; representations of animals)[60]).

Small soundings, necessitated by the construction of a new railway to Beersheba,
were made on the lower slopes at Tell Malat and Tel Milha uncovering superimposed paved approaches to the MC and MI gateways respectively in the former
case; and some fortifications of the MC and MI periods with a large area of round
pits full of white ashes (burned straw?) outside the walls, in the latter case.

Excavations at 'Afula headed by Dr. I. Ben-Dor and later by Dr. M. Dothan, shed
light on the Canaanite periods as well as on the transition to the Israelite period.
Among the interesting finds is a small structure of five stone slabs, two of them
stood on their edge, and three laid horizontally in front of the former, with an
adjacent stone socket (?) or rough bowl. The surface of the larger horizontal stone
is pitted with 20 small depressions arranged in three parallel rows. The stratum in
which these were found is dated to the EI period[61]).

A group of *tumuli* in the vicinity of Manahat (Malha) near Jerusalem has long been

---

[58]) Similar heaped sinkers covered with ash were also found in one Israelite layer (IV) at Tel "Gat".
[59]) Similar capitals, one of them ornamented on both faces, with a pillar intended to support such
a capital, were also found in the citadel at Hazor; Y. Yadin, BIES XXIII (1959), p. 24, pl. 4 (Hebrew).
[60]) Y. Aharoni, IEJ VI (1956), pp. 144 ff.
[61]) M. Dothan, 'Atiqot I (1955), pp. 19 ff.

a puzzle to archaeologists. Ever since Albright tried to excavate the largest of these from the top downwards, apparently despaired of reaching its base, and discontinued the excavation, the notion has spread that these were burial *tumuli*. Some archaeologists have never believed in this burial theory. In summer of 1953, a joint expedition of the Department of Antiquities and the IES, headed by Mrs. Ruth Amiran, proceeded to dismantle one of the larger *tumuli*. It was found that the *tumulus* itself consisted of a conical pile of packed rubble, almost without any admixture of earth, except for a small amount which had penetrated between the stones in the course of generations. Among the stones sherds were found which increased in number as the excavation progressed. All the sherds belong to the end of the period of the Kings, in the VIIIth-VIIth centuries B.C.E. At the base of the cone a 17-sided polygonal ringwall of undressed stone was found surrounding a rocky surface. Within this area, but off centre, were uncovered the remains of a pavement of flagstones, with a stone-lined hexagonal pit at its centre. In the south-eastern part of the surrounding wall was found an entrance consisting of a flight of steps leading up to the level of the pavement. Another opening was found almost opposite, in the south-western part of the surrounding wall. Several spots on the rock surface of the enclosed area showed deposits of ash and broken animal bones. A more or less similar state of affairs was uncovered in a second smaller *tumulus* nearby. A section cut on the edge of a third *tumulus* also revealed a polygonal surrounding wall. S. Yeivin therefore suggested that this was perhaps a group of pagan High-Places desecrated and stoned in the days of King Josiah[62].

Apart from individual graves and cemeteries mentioned above[63], belonging to the LI (Persian) period, only four excavations have touched strata belonging to this comparatively little known age. One, at Ayyelet Hashshahar has already been described.[64] At Hazor there were superimposed citadels of that period.[65] At Bet-Yerah, the series of campaigns conducted during 1951–1955 has revealed the presence of a hitherto unsuspected occupation dating to the IVth–IIIrd centuries B.C.E. in the southern part of the *tell*, characterized by a number of pottery (?) kilns with adjacent building remains sorely damaged by the overlying Hellenistic stratum.

Most interesting was a short exploratory excavation by N. Avigad of the Hebrew University, on behalf of the *Museum Haaretz* of Tel Aviv, at a small mound lying close to Tell Makmish on the sea shore, some five km. north of Tel Aviv. Badly ruined remains of a temple were uncovered, showing at least two phases of reconstruction. A comparatively large number of terracotta figurines was found.[66]

---

[62] R. Amiran, IEJ VIII (1958), pp. 1 ff.
[63] See above, p. 11.
[64] See above, p. 29.
[65] Y. Yadin et alii, *Hazor* I, pp. 48 ff.
[66] N. Avigad, BIES XXIII (1959), pp. 48 ff.

Similar figurines are in the hands of the Department of Antiquities from clandestine digging at this spot (pl. III, 4)[67].

## VII. *Excavations: Hellenistic-Byzantine Period*

Remains of the Hellenistic period were uncovered in several excavations. The deep sounding in the southern part of Bet-Yeraḥ was extended to a much larger area in the course of seasons 1951–1955, the upper layers investigated, and the topmost fortifications, belonging to the Hellenistic period, traced round the major part of the circumference of the *tell*. A large private house of the same period was uncovered; its walls were covered with layers of plaster above which was a thin white-wash painted over in wide coloured bands imitating stone panelling. The floors of the rooms were paved with a thick layer of hard cement mixed with potsherds, while the inner room had a large window in the east wall, opening to within some 30 cm. from the floor, looking out on the lake.

The city was encompassed by a heavy wall of mud-bricks erected on an understructure of basalt boulders, varying in thickness between 4 and 7 m. and some 3 m. high. Its main gateway has been swept away since a deep gully had formed there, but the foundations of the high protecting towers on either side were uncovered. The wall was further strengthened by a series of alternate round and square towers at approximately equal intervals (fig. 5).

A small fort apparently erected by the Hasmonean king Alexander Jannaeus was discovered near the sea-shore at Tel Aviv, with foundations of a hexagonal tower of the same period about one km. further east. These must have formed part of the defence line built according to Josephus by that king north of Jaffa[68].

A small Hasmonean fortress was the last vestige of occupation within the area of the citadel at Hazor[69].

Hellenistic tombs were uncovered at Shave Ziyyon on the sea-shore about 2.5 km south of Nehariyya, in which were pottery and Ptolemaic coins, proving the existence of the settlement of *Nea Kome* at that period.

Roman remains uncovered at Bet-Yeraḥ included some traces of a Roman military camp, which is probably to be assigned to Vespasian's army[70].

In Tiberias, an investigation of a badly ruined wall, in connection with a planned extension of a football playing field[71], undertaken by Mr. B. Ravani on behalf of the Department in 1953, led to six campaigns, in the course of which were revealed

---

[67]) See also above, p. 29 about the destroyed levels of the period at Tel "Gat" and ʾAyyelet Hashs shahar.

[68]) J. Kaplan, BIES XVII (1951), pp. 17 ff.

[69]) Y. Yadin et alii, *Hazor* I, pp. 63 ff.

[70]) Josephus, *Bell. Jud.*, VI, ix, 7.

[71]) The sports-ground was subsequently transferred to another place.

remains of the municipal baths, altered and reconstructed several times between the IVth and VIIIth centuries C.E. (originally located over an earlier public building of the IInd–IIIrd centuries C.E.), with partly preserved hypocausts, a number of built bath-tubs, mosaic paved halls, a subterranean cistern with reused columns and capitals, a whole series of water conduits, and a large number of small finds including marble incrustations (some of them gilded) for wall decorations, and fragmentary inscriptions (Aramaic and Greek).

Overlooking the eastern shore of Lake Gennezareth rises the steep and isolated hill crowned by the ruins of one of the fortified cities of the Decapolis, Susita (Hippos). In ancient times the main connection with the outside world was by the way of a narrow ridge leading eastwards. Here the Department investigated in 1952 the eastern gate of the city, opening at the end of the main thoroughfare. The excavations, directed by Miss Claire Epstein and Mr. E. Anati, revealed the basalt paved gateway, with the main water supplying conduit of stone pipes fitting into each other and laid under the pavement, and a semi-circular tower engaged in the city wall south of the gateway defending the approach to the latter. The whole dates to the IInd–IIIrd centuries C.E., and shows later reconstructions[72]).

An early investigation of the *tell* of Jaffa undertaken by the Department in 1950 under the direction of the late Lt.-Col. P.L.O. Guy, was later turned over to an expedition sent out by the University of Leeds under the direction of Dr. J. Bowman. The excavators reached virgin soil, and discovered that the trench is situated on the edge of the ancient *tell* and contains levels of the LI (Persian), Hellenistic (Hasmonean), Roman and Byzantine periods, the Middle Ages (XIIth–XIIIth centuries) and the XVIIIth–XIXth centuries. The main find, discovered in the course of Guy's excavations in 1950, was a hoard of coins from the days of king Alexander Jannaeus[73]).

A large farm building of the Roman period was unearthed near the painted tomb outside the city wall of Ascalon. A large hall connected with the farm was apparently dedicated to some oriental cult. A niche in the southern wall was paved in mosaics, in which was set an inscription ΑΥΞΙ ΤΡΑΙΑΝΕ. The place was investigated by Mr. Hevesi on behalf of the Department.

Mr. Hevesi also excavated another painted tomb in the vicinity. Only a small panel (showing a peacock and stylized plants) survived, and was removed (pl. VII, 3). Another tomb nearby was later (in Byzantine times) converted into a small bath-house. When the various springs in the Bet-She'an valley were cleaned and combined into one irrigation unit, a small installation was uncovered near 'Eyn Shoqeq ('Ayn Jausaq) consisting of ornamented stone benches arranged as a triclinium. The investigation was conducted by Mr. N. Zori on behalf of the Department.

---

[72]) 'Alon V–VI (1955), pp. 31–2 (Hebrew).
[73]) A. Kindler, IEJ IV (1954), pp. 170 ff., pls. 16–17. – The stratification at this spot decided Dr. Kaplan to start his investigation further east; see above pp. 25–26; 31.

The execution of development projects brought to light two Roman pottery kilns near Nehariyya (on the sea-shore) and Farwana (in the Bet-She'an valley). They were investigated on behalf of the Department by Dr. Z. Goldman and Mr. N. Zori respectively.

The main work in this period was concentrated on Jewish remains in the Judean desert. Because of the discovery of scrolls and other documents in Jordanian territory, a systematic search was conducted for caves in the territory of Israel. The Department of Antiquities has twice sent expeditions consisting mainly of volunteers from various agricultural settlements and students of the Hebrew University to the deep Ḥever Valley (Wady Ḥabra) in order to investigate its caves. Dr. Y. Aharoni directed the investigations. At the top of the precipice, one on each side of the deep canyon, were found two temporary Roman army camps overlooking and guarding two large caves in the rock-faces immediately beneath. The northern cave was investigated in the autumn of 1954. The openings led to a system of lofty halls penetrating for a length of some 150 m. into the heart of the mountain. The cave contained pottery, remnants of cloth and leather goods, shoes and soles, and remnants of wooden tools, all of which bore witness to the prolonged presence here of a large group of refugees in the IInd century C.E. The condition of the finds, however, showed that they had been recently disturbed, and empty Jordanian cigarette boxes indicated the nationality of the most recent ransackers.

Early in the summer of 1955, the southern cave was examined. It is 85 m. below the top of the precipice and about 250 m. above the valley floor, and is accessible only by a rope ladder. This cave too was found to penetrate 60 m. into the mountain, and the finds here also had been disturbed by Jordanian Bedawin; they were similar to the finds in the northern cave. In addition, a large number of skeletons was found, including some of women and children. They were apparently the remains of people who took refuge in this cave towards the end of the war of Bar-Kokheba, and died there of starvation, being unwilling to surrender to the Romans, but unable to leave because the cave was besieged by soldiers of the two camps above. Thus we find an unexpected confirmation of the historical truth of the tradition handed down to us in the Midrash[74]), the veracity and date of which was already discussed in the author's book on the *War of Bar-Kokheba*.

The second operation was a joint effort by all the organizations concerned with archaeology in Israel: the Department of Antiquities, the Hebrew University (Institute of Archaeology) and the IES. This joint expedition, directed by Dr. Y. Aharoni, Dr. N. Avigad and Dr. M. Avi-Yonah, embarked upon a systematic survey of Massada and made several soundings there, in order to ascertain whether and to what extent it would be now possible to undertake a large-scale expedition to uncover the ruins. In this expedition, too, took part volunteers (chiefly students and

---

[74]) *'Ekha Rabba* ch. I, § 16 (*Rom* edit., § 45).

agricultural settlers). First and foremost among them was Mr. Shemaryahu Gut-man, who has devoted many years to the investigation of the remains of Massada, and who discovered the sources of the water-supply, the „snake-path" and the ruins of Herod's palace. On Massada's flat top the expedition studied and corrected the plans of the ruins prepared by Schulten, and made a special study of the con-dition of the remains at the northern edge of the escarpment. They confirmed Gut-man's hypothesis that the place was Herod's palace, and uncovered its three main parts, built on the edge of the flat top and two lower ledges. On the summit of the escarpment, at the northern edge of Massada, evidently built by one of the Has-monean rulers, Jonathan or Johanan I, stood a spacious building with the oldest mosaic floors hitherto found in Israel. They were decorated with geometrical pat-terns. Herod improved and embellished this building, probably added a second storey, divided it from the remaining area of the fortress by a thick wall, and pos-sibly also added the semi-circular *exedra* in front. On a ledge of the rock, 20 m. be-low the summit, Herod built a peculiar structure. Here, two concentric walls pro-truded from the debris: they were never any higher, for their tops are finished off and coped. At one point the space between them was cleared, revealing a plastered floor at a depth of 3.40 m. As the space between the walls has not been completely cleared, the nature of this round structure is not yet clear. A hidden staircase, in-visible to the outside observer, was hewn within the vertical rock face, and con-tained flights of steps spiralling round a central pillar. The lower steps were cut in the rock, and the higher ones were originally made of wood. This staircase com-municated between the palace on the escarpment and the first ledge; a similar structure connected this ledge with another one twelve meters below. Here sup-porting walls were erected on three sides of the rocky ledge, lining the precipitous slopes of the natural terrace. On the east and west they encompassed just below the levels of the ledge vaulted cellars not yet explored. Above these, a courtyard was laid out surrounded by a roofed portico, supported on columns with Corin-thian capitals, 4 m. high. The stems of the columns were built of drums of friable sandstone, covered on the outside with a thick layer of plaster in which were moulded the flutings of the columns, the details of the bases and the ornamentation of the capitals. Some of these magnificent columns still stand to their full height (pl. IV, 2). The rock wall at the rear was also plastered, and painted to imitate veined marble. The whole structure agrees amazingly with the detailed description given by Josephus[75]. All these buildings bear signs of the great fire which destroyed this stronghold of the last zealots, when it was taken by the Romans[76]).
The results of this survey were discussed by the Committee of Scientists for the Advancement of Archaeological Research, which represents the three Israeli ar-

---

[75]) Josephus, *Bell. Jud.* VII, viii, 3.
[76]) M. Avi-Yonah, N. Avigad, Y. Aharoni et alii, IEJ VII (1957), pp. 1 ff.

chaeological organizations. It was decided not to continue with large-scale excavation and research until such time as definite steps could be taken to ensure conservation of the uncovered ruins.

However, volunteers working under the guidance of Mr. Sh. Gutman improved the „snake-path" leading to the top of Massada, so that the ascent can be made now with comparative ease. With his enthusiasm and zeal Mr. Y. Almog, chairman of the regional council of Sedom, has succeeded in erecting a comfortable youth hostel at the foot of the rock; and with the help of the Government Tourist Corporation[77]) it is intended to undertake conservation work in the nearby Roman camps. It should be stated here most emphatically that the operations in the Hever valley and at Massada would have been absolutely impossible without the generous help of the Israel Defence Army, from the then Chief of Staff and his high-ranking officers, through the local commanders, down to the privates who took part in the expeditions.

Further north the oasis of 'Eyn Gedi was investigated at first by an expedition of the IES led by Professor B. Mazar in 1949. It was found that *Tell Jurn* was a natural hillock, and only some remains of ancient buildings were scattered over its surface here and there. On the top of the mound were remains of a small fortress. A trial trench in one of its corners proved that it is to be dated to the Roman and Byzantine periods, but it was erected over the ruins of an earlier MI fort. The explorers concluded that the oasis had never contained a concentrated permanent settlement, only several forts and watch-towers, at various strategic points. The agriculturers must have lived in temporary shelters scattered throughout the oasis. All available arable land was put to use, properly terraced, and during all periods great care was taken of the proper storage and distribution of both spring and flood waters[78]). The survey of the area was continued under the auspices of the Department and the IES, being led by Mr. J. Naveh, who also undertook a small trial dig in one of the temporary building remains on the slope overlooking the creek on the north, where he discovered under the debris of the Roman occupation, remains of a small Chalcolithic settlement[79]).

The renewed excavations of the IES at Bet-She'arim, which yielded such an abundance of material illustrating Jewish life, art and funerary architecture and rites in the IIIrd–VIIth centuries C.E., have already been described[80]).

Various soundings in Jerusalem brought to light remains of the Roman, Byzantine and Crusader periods. Particular interest attaches to the soundings in the area of the Qirya (Giv'at Ram), where a built up area of the Herodian period was later converted into a brickyard of the Tenth Legion. The soundings were directed by Dr.

[77]) See below, p. 53.
[78]) B. Maisler, BJPES XV, 1–2 (1949/50), pp. 25 ff. (Hebrew).
[79]) A report on this investigation by J. Naveh is being published now by the Dept.
[80]) See above, pp. 6–9.

Avi-Yonah for the Department and the IES. Nearby, the remains of a church with partly preserved mosaic floors were revealed; it was dedicated (as stated in a Greek inscription) to St. George. The fact that such a church existed somewhere in the vicinity was known from contemporary sources (VIth–VIIth cent. C.E.)[81]. Some distance away, labourers employed by the Qirya Office, under the direction of the Department, cleared the remains of a Byzantine nymphaeon containing large mosaic-paved tanks, which supplied water to fountains in the form of half-domed niches. The half-domed ceilings of the niches were plastered over and moulded into conch-shells. These fountains drained into a mosaic-paved square, which contained central water-cisterns. The remains of a second nymphaeon were discovered on the slopes of the hill over-looking the Monastery of the Cross on the west. These remains were excavated by Mr. L. Y. Rahmani. In the Har Hammenuhot cemetery two structures were uncovered which were probably small forts, with attached farms, overlooking the old Roman road from Jerusalem to Moza. One of these was excavated by Mrs. Ruth Amiran [82] and the other by Mr. J. Leibovitch[83]. The remains of an industrial quarter were uncovered north of the Crusader wall in Byzantine Rishpon (Apollonia): there were wine and olive presses and, more particularly, remains of several furnaces used for glassmaking. Glassmaking was a flourishing industry in the early Arab period. The excavation was directed by Dr. I. Ben-Dor and later by Dr. P. Kahane.[84]

In the near neighbourhood of Nethanya were unearthed several industrial and agricultural installations among them dyeworks. The soundings were directed by Dr. F. Berger and the late Y. Ory.

The Department of Antiquities has carried out, under the direction of Mr. N. Zori, a number of interesting soundings in the Byzantine city buried under the new town of Bet-She'an. In one place remains of buildings were found in superimposed layers, dating from the IVth–VIIth centuries C.E. All the buildings seem to have been residential. In Layer B from the bottom were uncovered remains of a peristyle court, while in Layer D was found part of a paved road. A hoard of coins in a jug buried under a floor in Layer C deserves special mention. It contained 405 minimi dating from the IVth–Vth centuries C.E.[85]

At Shikkun Aleph, a new housing quarter north of the police station, a large mansion 27 x 32 m was unearthed, dating from the Vth–VIth centuries C.E. The mansion had at least eighteen „rooms", among them a large courtyard with stairs leading to a second storey. An ancient lavatory in this court was connected to a drain,

---

[81]) M. Avi-Yonah, BIES XV (1949), pp. 19 ff., pls VI–VII.
[82]) Ruth Amiran, 'Alon III (1951), pp. 43–4, pl. V, 2–3.
[83]) J. Leibovitch, Ibid. V–VI (1957), pp. 24–5.
[84]) J. Ben-Dor and P. Kahane, Ibid. III (1951), pp. 41–3, pls. VI, 2–3; VII, 2–3.
[85]) N. Zori, Ibid. V–VI (1957), pp. 16–19, pls. I–II, 1.

and another vertical drain in an adjoining wall no doubt led from a lavatory on the second floor. On the ground floor a group of rooms open to visitors could be recognized, most of them paved in mosaics of rather large white tesserae. In one of the walls, near the entrance to an inside room, was a semi-circular niche, paved with similar mosaic tesserae; near it was a hole in the floor, leading into a drain. In another inside room a small square fountain was built against the rear wall. It was about 60 cm. high, and was originally coped with white marble. Water was supplied by a narrow lead pipe running through the wall, and connected on the outside to a pottery pipe forming part of the elaborate and ramified water-supply system. Above the lead pipe in the inside room was the plastered and white washed floor of a niche which originally may have contained the ikon of a saint. There were in fact many indications that the owners of the house were Christians. Another group of rooms discovered comprised various kitchen and household appurtenances and storerooms. Hundreds of small finds were unearthed all over the house: various types of pottery vessels; bronze and pottery lamps; stands for bronze lamps; weights; other household ware; a bronze knocker for the outer gate; a white glass cameo, fashioned in white on a dark background, depicting perhaps some Hellenistic ruler. The cameo was no doubt a precious heirloom, handed down from generation to generation. Especially interesting was a collection of iron sickles, scythe, woodcutting implements, ploughshares, and hoes, which, had they not been found here in a deep sealed layer, might have been considered modern. A deep sounding made in one of the rooms showed that the house had been repaired and renovated several times. Outside the building, on virgin soil, were scanty remains of a Chalcolithic settlement[86]).

Other soundings in the city, also directed by N. Zori on behalf of the Department, brought to light remains of the Byzantine city wall, large baths with an adjoining building paved in mosaics, and remains of a room with a complete mosaic floor in a different house.

The most extensive exploration of Byzantine remains was undertaken by the Department at Caesarea, under the direction of S. Yeivin. Here, during the clearing of a large stone heap in one of the fields, near the bend of the road southwards to Kibbuz Sedot Yam, was found a huge, damaged, red porphyry statue. Excavations at this spot and a sounding made at the edge of the road nearby revealed the following stratification, from the surface downwards:

A.   A stratum belonging to the XIth–XIIIth centuries C.E. This layer had been badly disturbed, for after the collapse of the buildings generation after generation pillaged their stones, and during the last decades much of the area has been under cultivation.

B.   A second stratum, dated to the VIIIth–Xth centuries C.E., also somewhat

---

[86]) A full report on the excavations of this villa is being published in 'Atiqot III.

disturbed owing to building operations in the level above it. The relationship be-tween the two is not sufficiently clear. Traces of a big fire are visible in many places. It seems, therefore, reasonable to assume that this level of occupation was destroy-ed by fire, possibly as a result of a conquest of the town.

C.    A Late Byzantine layer (Vth–VIIth centuries C.E.), consisting mainly of a large built-up area. This includes a long courtyard paved with marble slabs which had undoubtedly been pillaged from monumental buildings of earlier periods. So far the courtyard measures over 30 m.; the southern end has not yet been uncovered. Certain arrangements here suggest that this may have been the central *livestock market* of the town.

On the north the „courtyard" leads to a tripartite opening, flanked on either side by a statue, about two and half times life-size. By artistic criteria the marble statue on the west may be dated to the IInd–IIIrd century C.E., antedating by far the building in which it was found; while the red porphyry (undoubtedly Egyptian) statue, seated on a granite chair, may be dated to the IIIrd–IVth century C.E. (pl. V, 1).

The tripartite entrance led into a rectangular room paved with a fairly rough mo-saic inlaid with simple geometrical patterns. Doorways led to adjacent rooms on the east and west. The eastern section of the north wall was missing, and its place was taken by a monumental stairway of ten broad and shallow steps, at the foot of which was inlaid in the mosaic floor a six-lined Greek inscription, set in a *tabula ansata*. The inscription mentions a hitherto unknown governor of the province. The above mentioned flight of steps leads to a northbound street, 1.50 m. higher than the floor of the "livestock market" and the room to its north. The street is 8 m. wide, and 22 m. of its length have so far been exposed, but traces of it have been discovered at a corresponding depth in a trial trench sunk about 80 m. north of the main excavation. The whole street is paved with mosaics, the geometrical designs of which are similar to those in the room south of the staircase. There were small shops and workshops on its eastern side at least, one of which belonged to a craftsman in stone, who made stone incrustations for the ornamentation of walls. Several examples of such incrustations were found. The side room on the east of the inscription (see above) opens through a tripartite entrance onto a marble paved court running eastwards, which has not yet been cleared.[87]

D.    An investigation of a hole in a pavement of the "market" showed the existence of a long stone wall running diagonally across the market (under the pavement), which could be dated by the style of its masonry to the Roman period.

Badly ruined remains of a late Roman theatre were uncovered near the sea-shore immediately north of the *tell* at Dor.[88]

---

[87] S. Yeivin, Archaeology VIII (1955), pp. 122 ff.
[88] J. Leibovitch, 'Alon III (1954), pp. 38–9, pl. IV, 2.

Part of a stone understructure of an additional aqueduct, possibly leading to Caesarea, but never completed, were unearthed near Binyamina.[89]

## VIII. *Excavations: Buildings for Religious Purposes*

Discovery and research in the field of ritual and religious buildings in Israel form a chapter on their own. During the period under review eight ancient synagogues previously unknown have been registered, five of which have been explored. A late type was discovered at Bet-Yeraḥ, an intermediate one at Yafia'. Then there is the Samaritan synagogue at Sha'albim (Salbit). The remains at Kh. Shura, Kh. Muntar, and Kh. el-Mujeydilat have not yet been investigated. A building discovered at Khirbet Ruqqadiyye near Hulda, which no doubt served ritual purposes, also belongs to this group. It is rectangular, is facing north and contains two rooms with undecorated mosaic floors composed of fairly large white cubes. It was excavated by Mr. Y. Ory. Pairs of niches, protruding on the outside, were built in the three external walls of the north room. In the middle of the south room was a round cistern with plastered walls, a mosaic paved floor, and two semi-circular steps at the bottom. On its east side and connected with it by a conduit was a more shallow, square cistern. The mosaic pavement of the southern room shows that the cisterns were dug when the building was erected and are not the result of a later reconstruction. The entrance to the building was in the short south wall, where the threshold stone was found. Inside, set in the mosaic floor, was a somewhat diagonally inset rectangular tablet which exhibits on the left a *lulav* inserted at its base into a plaited palm-leaf sheath; on the right is portrayed a seven-branched *candelabrum* on three legs with lighted lamps on top, surrounded by a *shofar*, a snuff-shovel and an *ethrog*. Above, between the *lulav* and the *candelabrum*, is a Greek inscription: *Praise unto the people.* East of this tablet a circle was inset into the mosaic floor containing a Greek inscription with the names of the donors picked out in red tesserae. The rest of the inscription is in black tesserae. If it were not for the tablet depicting ritual objects and the dedicatory inscription, one would not have hesitated to classify the building as yet another wine or olive press. However, the religious adornment necessarily leads to the conclusion that the building was designed for certain religious purposes, and it may therefore be taken to be a *miqva*, or ritual bath. In 1949 soldiers of the Israel Defence Army stationed at Sha'albim (Salbit) informed the Department of Antiquities of the discovery there of mosaics. These turned out to be remains of a Samaritan synagogue, which was excavated by the late Professor E. L. Sukenik on behalf of the Archaeological Institute of the Hebrew University. Here was uncovered a building oriented towards Mount Gerizim and paved with

---

[89] Ibid., p. 10, pl. V, 1.

variegated mosaics showing several patterns of ornamentation. The synagogue was built in the IVth century C.E., was apparently ruined during the Samaritan risings at the end of the century, and restored in the Vth century. The building finally fell into ruin, it seems, in the course of the VIth century[90]).

A synagogue at Yafia' (Yafa) near Nazareth was excavated in 1950 under the direction of the late Professor E. L. Sukenik on behalf of the same Institute. This turned out to be an ordinary basilica of the intermediary type, facing east, apparently on the assumption that the territory of Zebulun is in the western part of the country; its entrance was on the west through a porch in front of the main hall. The building was paved with ornamental mosaics. In the central nave were preserved the remains of a large circle, within which were inlaid small contiguous circles. Remains of two animal figures and a fragmentary inscription accompanying one of them have led the late excavator to the conclusion that the floor of the synagogue had been inlaid with a circle showing the symbols of the tribes instead of the Zodiac[91]). Professor M. Avi-Yonah excavated on behalf of the same Institute the synagogue situated on the sea-shore at Caesarea, north of the harbour. There remains had first been noticed in 1945, and partly investigated by the late Y. Ory, revealing some mosaic floors with Greek inscriptions[92]). Avi-Yonah uncovered the main building, where he was able to distinguish three phases of reconstruction from the IVth to the VIth centuries C.E.

The investigations carried out by the Archaeological Institute of the Hebrew University in the synagogues of Sha'albim, Yafia' and Caesarea were financed by the Louis M. Rabinowitz Fund for the Exploration of Ancient Synagogues.

The largest synagogue (23 x 37 m) so far investigated in Israel is that of Tel Bet-Yerah[93]). In the northern part of the *tell* north of the baths was uncovered an enclosure 60 x 60 metres (fig. 5). Its walls were built of ashlar and at the four corners were four small turrets which had apparently been originally domed; their interior walls or ceilings were decorated with mosaics of coloured glass cubes. Some of the glass cubes were also gilded. Two similar turrets were built on both sides of the main entrance, in the middle of the southern wall. One of these was dismantled and removed during the excavations in 1945-6, in order to reach underlying layers. This building was not erected before the IVth century C.E., but its original purpose has not yet been clarified. Probably towards the end of the Vth century, a large synagogue of a late type was built in the middle of the enclosed area. Its entrance is on the north, and in the south wall a semi-circular apse is oriented to-

---

[90]) E. L. Sukenik, Bulletin of the Louis M. Rabinowitz Fund for the Exploration of Ancient Synagogues I (1949), pp. 25 ff.; II (1951), pp. 27-8.

[91]) Idem, Bulletin II (1951), pp. 6 ff.

[92]) Idem, Bulletin I (1949), pls. X-XI; II (1951), pp. 28-30, pls. XIII-XVI.

[93]) On the circumstances under which this dig was initiated see above, p. 20; cf. P. L. O. Guy, 'Alon III (1951), pp. 32-3, pl. II, 1-2.

wards Jerusalem. The floors of the synagogue itself and the adjoining rooms on the west were paved with coloured mosaics, but as this area was later cultivated and the remains of the synagogue were very close to the surface, only isolated fragments of the pavement have survived; among them is one of a bird near a citron (ethrog) tree in fruit. On a base of a column found in the area were incised a menora, a ram's horn, a citron and a snuff-shovel. These are the ritual utensils commonly shown in synagogue decoration. When the synagogue was built, an entrance was probably opened in the north wall of the enclosure for a two-leaved door, in front of which a very shallow stone tank was placed, perhaps for the washing of hands and feet, and it is possible that a long narrow portico was paved along the outer side of the wall. A ramified network of channels and clay water pipes supplied water to the building and allowed rainwater to drain.

In the course of road building operations near Nirim (at Ḥorvat Maʻon) in the Western Negev were revealed remains of a mosaic floor. The Department delegated Mr. S. Levy to investigate. His excavation laid bare an ancient synagogue of a very peculiar construction. It was properly oriented to the NNE (towards Jerusalem), with an apsis at that end of the central nave; here were uncovered a deep depression for the treasury of the synagogue, as well as certain bone incrustations and fittings which probably have originally adorned a wooden Ark of the Law that stood in the niche. In the immediate vicinity were also found several small sheets of bronze rolled up into tubes which bear engraved Greek (?) inscriptions.[94]

The apse may have been separated from the main part of the building by a curtain hung on marble colonettes[95] (thrown up in the course of road building). A small area paved in plain mosaics between the apse and the central nave is lower than the rest of the floor, a quite common custom in several comparatively modern synagogues, as a symbol of the verse: Out of the depths have I called thee, Oh Lord[96]), for here stood the precentor who led the congregation in prayer. At the northern end of the central nave a garbled Aramaic inscription in a tabula ansata is included in the mosaic pavement commemorating the whole community, who contributed the money for the mosaic and singling out for especial mention three people who gave a crown (חג; for the Scroll of the Law) worth two dinars.

The central nave was paved with an ornamented and coloured mosaic floor, most of the western part of which had been destroyed before the beginning of the excavations; this, however, was not an irreparable loss, as it was obvious that the designs were absolutely symmetrical on both sides of a central strip, and could be easily reconstructed on the basis of the almost complete eastern half (pl. VI, 1). On the east side the mosaic floor of the central nave abuts on a row of square

---

[94] Not unrolled as yet and hence undeciphered.
[95] Cf. the curtains drawn apart to reveal the ark and candelabra, in the mosaic floor of the synagogue of Bet ʼAlpha (E. L. Sukenik, The Ancient Synagogue of Beth-Alpha, Jerusalem, 1932, pl. 8).
[96] Ps. 130 : 1.

foundations for pillars (or columns?), and beyond them the eastern aisle is paved with small rectangular slabs of limestone, this regular pavement extending far to the east up to a small ablution installation, as well as to the north beyond the line of the apse. Only on the south there are remains of a stone wall with a central entrance leading into the nave. On the west there are remains of a pavement similar to the eastern one without any traces of a west wall. On the north, too, there were no traces of an enclosing wall.

The mosaics are very vivid and well executed. They closely resemble in contents and layout those of a Byzantine church uncovered in 1917, which are dated to 561/2 C.E.[97]. They may have been laid by the same artisan[97a].

In the ruins of ʿAlma was found the second half of a lintel from the ancient synagogue of this village, which completed the inscription on the long known first half.[98] Its interest lies in the fact that it definitely proves the use of the Aramaic דעבד (deʿaved) as actually meaning *made*, *fashioned*, and not merely *donated* as it could be, and actually had been, translated in all previously known dedicatory inscriptions. A fragment of another inscription from the same ancient synagogue was discovered in 1949[99].

A second group of religious buildings includes Christian churches and monasteries of the Byzantine period. Twenty-nine ancient churches, chapels, monasteries, and monastic farms have been discovered. They are, from south to north; a prayer chapel in the ruins of a small miners' settlement on a tributary of Naḥal Roded in the Negev (notification by Mr. Y. Braslavski of the Friends of the Department of Antiquities)[100]; vestiges of a church in the vicinity of Massuʿot Yizḥaq; a chapel at Barneaʿ, north of Ascalon (excavated by Mr. Y. Ory); a Byzantine church paved with mosaics at ʿAgur in the hills SW of Jerusalem, where were found indications of a gallery over the side aisles (excavated by Mr. R. Gofna); a Byzantine church paved with mosaics at Roglit (Kh. Jurfa; pl. V, 3), in the hills SW of Jerusalem (excavated by Miss V. Zwilichovsky); a small mosaic paved church at Ozem (Kh. Beyt Mamin), some 15 km. east of Ascalon (excavated by Mr. R. Gofna); a large mosaic paved church at the southern Hazor (Kh. Banaya; excavated by the late Y. Ory); a monastic farm with a prayer chapel and a well built tomb under the courtyard at Ruhama (excavated by Mr. R. Gofna); St. George's Church in Jerusalem[101]; a mortuary chapel at Bet-Ṣafafa south-west of Jerusalem (excavated by Mr. Y. H. Landau) with a mosaic floor, containing in an alcove on the west side an inscription of four lines, reading backwards from bottom to top; in a nearby underground

---

[97] A. D. Trendall, *The Shellal Mosaic*, Canberra, 1957, p. 13.
[97a] EI VI (1960), pp. 77 ff.
[98] Cf. S. Klein, *Sefer Hayyishuv* I, Jerusalem, 1930, p. 122, pl. 16, 2.
[99] Ruth Amiran, ʿAlon II (1950), pp. 25-6, pl. IV, 4.
[100] J. Braslavsky, *Studies in Our Country, its Past and Remains*, Tel Aviv, 1954, p. 298.
[101] See above, pp. 38–39.

tomb were found six lead coffins decorated with crosses, four for adults and two for children[102]); a church and monastery at Khirbet Ṣaleḥ, near Ramat Raḥel[103]); a Late Byzantine church at Kefar Truman paved with mosaics (excavated by Miss V. Zwilichovski); a church near Kefar Syrkin (partly excavated by Mr. J. Kaplan for the Department of Antiquities); a church at Baḥan (excavated by the late Y. Ory); a large open air church in the cemetery outside the walls of Caesarea with variegated mosaics portraying birds and quadrupeds (pl. V, 2) as well as a profusion of geometric designs (excavated by S. Yeivin); a church on the lower course of the Crocodilion river (notification by Mr. A. Wegman of the Friends of the Department); a church at Dor (excavated by Mr. J. Leibovitch)[104]); a church with mosaic floors at Kh. Damun on Mount Carmel (notification by the prison superintendent there); the remains of a monastery with mosaic floors, richly decorated with plants and animals designs and bearing two Greek inscriptions, near Sha'ar Ha'aliya (excavated by Dr. M. Dothan)[105]); a large church at 'Evron with a profusion of mosaics containing a variety of decorations and inscriptions (ten in Greek and one in Syriac), giving the dates of construction and repairs during the Vth century C.E. (excavated successively by Messrs. Dr. M. Avi-Yonah, Dr. P. Kahane and Y. H. Landau)[106]); an early Byzantine church paved with mosaics at Shave Zion (excavated by Mr. M. Prausnitz); a church at Ḥanita (excavated by Mr. M. Prausnitz); a church and *baptisterium* with variegated mosaic floors containing four inscriptions in Greek and one in Syriac and Greek, on the northern part of the Tel Bet-Yeraḥ[107]); a monastic farm containing two rooms with decorated mosaic floor, dedicated to prayer, near Bet Hashshiṭṭa (excavated by Dr. Y. Aharoni)[108]); a church and monastery with mosaic pavements and foundations for a belfry at Sede Naḥum (excavated by Mr. N. Zori); and at least three churches and one baptismal chapel at Hippos – Susita where Dr. M. Avi-Yonah excavated one church[109]), and Miss C. Epstein and Mr. E. Anati excavated another church and the baptistery nearby[110]). In addition, a fragmentary mosaic showing a pair of (a bishop's) sandals uncovered under one of the modern houses of Beersheba (in the course of repairs) may belong to remains of a church; a large mosaic paved building at Baikat 'Umm Huseyn (near Nirim) seems to represent the ruins of a church (not yet investigated). The colourfulness and rich *repertoire* of motives of the Israel mosaics have interested

---

[102]) Y. Landau, 'Alon V–VI (1957), pp. 40–2, pl. V, 3; M. Avi-Yonah, loc. cit., p. 43.
[103]) See above, p. 32.
[104]) J. Leibovitch,, 'Alon V–VI (1957), p. 35, pl. V, 2.
[105]) M. Dothan, IEJ V (1955), pp. 96 ff., pls. 19–20.
[106]) M. Avi-Yonah, P. Kahane, Y. Landau, 'Alon V–VI (1957), pp. 34–5, pl. V, 1.
[107]) See below, p. 50.
[108]) Y. Aharoni, *Excavations at Beth-Hashitta*, BIES XVIII (1954), pp. 209 ff.
[109]) A. Shulman, 'Alon V–VI (1957), pp. 30–31.
[110]) E. Anati, Ibid., pp. 31–33., pls. IV, 3–4, VI, 1; M. Avi-Yonah, Ibid., p. 33.

Unesco, who decided to dedicate a volume of the Unesco World Art Series to Israel mosaics. P. Bellew (director), M. Dolfi (photographer) and A. Schutz (of the New York Graphic Society) visited Israel in the summer of 1958 and with the cooperation of the Department took coloured photographs of a large number of mosaics. The volume is due to be published towards the end of 1960.

## IX. *Archaeological Surveys*

From its earliest days, the Department of Antiquities has paid particular attention to the need for a comprehensive archaeological survey of the country.

The late P.L.O. Guy already started such a survey on behalf of the PEF in 1937, but his work was interrupted by the Second World War.

Then, again, in the summer 1949 the IES in active collaboration with the Department of Antiquities presented the Government with a detailed memorandum on the proposed survey, which was to be undertaken by all the archaeological institutions in the country. Owing to lack of funds and unavailability of properly trained archaeologists in sufficient numbers, neither Guy's large scale programme nor the proposals of the IES could be implemented. But partial surveys are being made in various areas. Mr. N. Zori has made a detailed survey of the Jordan Valley, between the frontier and the Sea of Galilee, the Bet-She'an (Beisan) Valley, and the north-eastern part of the Gilboa' mountains which lies in Israel[111]. The Haifa archaeological circle, especially Messrs. Dubbi, Wreschner, Olamy and Fraenkel, is engaged on a detailed survey of Mount Carmel, with particular reference to prehistoric remains[112]. Dr. J. Kaplan has made a detailed survey of the municipal area of Tel Aviv and its surroundings[113]. Dr. M. Dothan of the Dept. surveyed the area round Yavne Yam[114]. The archaeological circle of the Committee for Cultural Work affiliated to the Tel Aviv Workers' Council, under the direction of Mr. S. Avizur, is continually making partial surveys in the Sharon and the Shephela[115]. Professor Mazar and his students had made partial surveys in various parts of the Shephela (the low foot-hills of Judea). As a result, it was suggested by Y. Aharoni and Ruth Amiran that Tell Nagila should be identified with 'Eglon[116]. Mazar suggested the identification of Ras 'Abu Ḥumeyd with Gittaim[117]. Mr. D. Alon of Mishmar Hannegev who had continually been surveying the southern Shephela and the northern Ne-

---

[111]) N. Zori, BIES XVIII (1954), pp. 78 ff.; XIX (1955), pp. 89 ff.

[112]) A report by Y. Olami on such a survey is to be published in 'Atiqot III; for a partial report by Y. Wreschner, see 'Alon V–VI (1957), pp. 49 ff.

[113]) J. Kaplan, RB LXII (1955), pp. 92 ff., and see above, p. 13.

[114]) M. Dothan, IEJ II (1952), pp. 104–112.

[115]) The results of this survey have not yet been published.

[116]) Ruth Amiran and Y. Aharoni, BIES XVII (1952), pp. 52 ff.

[117]) B. Mazar, IEJ IV (1954), pp. 227 ff.

gev, has discovered most of the Chalcolithic settlements which were subsequently excavated, and has suggested that Tel Haror (Tell 'Abu Hureyra) be identified with Gerar of the Age of the Patriarchs.[118] Mr. E. Anati for the Department of Antiquities, with the active help of a group of amateurs from Sede Boqer and Revivim, has been engaged on a survey of the northern and central Negev. This led to the discovery of an ancient road from Tell 'Arad to the oasis of Qadesh Barnea' ('Eyn Qudeyrat), defended by a chain of small forts dating to the Israelite period. Also discovered were many groups of drawings – single or composite – engraved on rocks[119]. These belong to different periods; many are accompanied by graffiti in Thamudic[120], Safaitic[121], and early Kufic scripts. A more systematic and comprehensive activity was undertaken in Galilee under the auspices of the Department of Antiquities and headed by Dr. Y. Aharoni with the active help of a circle of amateurs, mostly Trustees of the Department. As a results of this survey, which is still in progress, new facts were brought to light concerning Israelite settlements in northern Galilee in the days of the Judges. In connection with these, soundings were made at Qadesh in Galilee and Horvat Harashim (Khirbet Tuleyl)[122].

Mr. E. Anati, while on the staff of the Department, carried out also a partial survey in the area of Nahal 'Iron (Wady 'Ara), which resulted in the discovery of a series of small MI forts.

Mr. L. Y. Rahmani of the Department is carrying out a detailed survey of the 'Adullam area SW of Jerusalem, where he discovered some new sites and was able to obtain interesting sketch-plans and information on long known ones.

Mr. J. Naveh of the Department made a detailed study of Tell el-Muqanna'[123]; and together with Mr. R. Gofna surveyed the area between Tel Ashdod and Ashdod Yam.

Mr. M. Meir, of Qibbuz Gal'ed and one of the Trustees of the Friends of Antiquities made a detailed survey of his neighbourhood.

Miss E. Yeivin of the Department is engaged in a full registration and classification of local collections of prehistoric antiquities, mainly flint artifacts, coupled with a survey of adjacent sites.

The Botanical Department of the Hebrew University under the direction of Professor M. Evenari, is carrying out a survey of ancient agriculture in various areas of the Negev; Dr. Y. Aharoni takes care of the archaeological aspects of this survey[124]. Only one full scale survey of a definite large area, namely the Negev, has been

---

[118]) D. 'Alon, Mibbifnim XVI, 1 (1952), pp. 46 ff.
[119]) Cf. e.g., E. Anati, PEQ 87 (1955), pp. 49 ff.
[120]) F. V. Winnett, Atiqot II (1959), pp. 146 ff.
[121]) A. Jame, Ibid., pp. 150 ff.
[122]) See above, pp. 26–27 and note 44.
[123]) J. Naveh, IEJ VIII (1958), pp. 87 ff., 165 ff.
[124]) M. Evenari, Y. Aharoni, L. Shannan, N. H. Tadmor, IEJ VIII (1958), pp. 231 ff.

undertaken so far. This was recently completed by Professor Nelson Glueck of the
Hebrew Union College, with the funds provided by the late Louis M. Rabinowitz.
His survey has shown that the Negev was cultivated and fairly densely populated
in the Chalcolithic-Middle Canaanite and Israelite periods, but especially from
Nabatean times until the Arab conquest[125]).

## X.  *Excavations: Foreign Expeditions*

The above account details archaeological work carried out in Israel by the Department of Antiquities and Israeli bodies: The Archaeological Institute of the Hebrew
University[126]), The Department of Prehistory of that Institute[127]), The Israel exploration Society[128]), the James de Rothschild's Expedition[129]), the Museum
Ha'arez[130]), frequently supported by municipal or local councils, mainly Tel
Aviv[131]), but also Jerusalem[132]), Haifa[133]), Beersheba, Ascalon, Netanya, Nehariyya,
and Tiberias.

From its inception, the Department of Antiquities has tried to encourage scientific
institutions abroad to renew their archaeological work in Israel. In order to over-
come the difficulty of high labour costs in Israel, as compared with neighbouring
countries, the Director of the Department of Antiquities, with the approval of
Mr. M. Sharett, the then acting minister of Education and Culture, published in
1951 an open letter in the Palestine Exploration Quarterly, in which he offered
every foreign archaeological expedition a subsidy amounting to 2/3 of its expendi-
ture on actual wages, up to a maximum of 2,000 work-days per season.

A French expedition excavated in Israel for the first time in the autumn 1950. The
slope north of the village of Qaryat el-ʿAnab was investigated on behalf of the
French *Commission des fouilles* under the direction of the late René Neuville, and
the remains of a poor Neolithic settlement were found. Its culture was linked with
the flint implements of el-Khiyam on the one hand, of Jericho on the other[134]).
Since 1952, an expedition of the *Centre national de la recherche scientifique* under the
direction of M. Jean Perrot has been excavating Chalcolithic settlements at Be'er

[125]) A popular account of this survey has been recently published by N. GLUECK, *Rivers in the Desert*, New York, 1959.
[126]) See above, 1; 32–34; 36–38; 42–43.
[127]) See above, p. 12.
[128]) See above, 31–33; 38–39.
[129]) See above, p. 27.
[130]) See above, p. 33.
[131]) See above, pp. 25–26; 31–32.
[132]) See below, p. 51.
[133]) See above, p. 46, and below, p. 52.
[134]) J. Perrot, 'Alon III (1951), p. 28; id., Syria XXXIX (1952), pp. 119 ff.

Raqiq, Be'er Maṭar and Be'er Ẓafad, all of them along the Beersheba creek or its confluents[135]).

In 1952 an expedition sponsored by the University of Leeds and directed by Dr. J. Bowman, examined the edges of the *tell* of ancient Jaffa[136]).

An expedition of the Oriental Institute of the University of Chicago, under the direction of Professor P. Delougaz, excavated in the winter of 1952–53 an area in the northern part of Tel Bet-Yeraḥ. Here the expedition uncovered a large structure paved with basalt flagstones from the EA period round VIIIth–IXth centuries C.E. This was no doubt a continuation of the large structure discovered south of this area during the excavations of the Department of Antiquities. Underneath it, was uncovered a large Christian basilica with a baptistery nearby[137]). One of the inscriptions in the mosaic floor fixes the date of construction as 528/9 C.E. An interesting point is that the date is not given according to the era in use at Tiberias, but conforms to the era used at Hippos (Susita), which shows that the place was at that time part of Transjordan, meaning that the Jordan then flowed west of the Tell in its old bed, which is still visible (cf. fig. 5). A trial trench reaching virgin soil showed that underneath the church lay a level of settlement of the Roman period, and beneath that, levels belonging to the various stages of the EC period. The expedition also cleared several tombs in the Byzantine cemetery.

In 1955 Father B. Bagatti excavated on behalf of the Custodia di Terra Santa at Nazareth the building site of the new Church of Annunciation; he uncovered the remains of an earlier Crusaders' church and below it a Byzantine basilica[138]).

Early in 1958 a survey team of Italian archaeologists connected with the *Istituto Lombardo di Scienze e Lettere*, Milano, led by Professor Doro Levi, visited Israel to investigate possibilities of excavations at Caesarea. As a result of this visit an expedition sponsored by the abovementioned Institute, under the direction of Professor L. Crema, with Dr. A. Frova as director-in-the-field is digging at Caesarea (as from the spring 1959).

Negociations are also conducted with other Italian, U.K. and U.S.A. learned Societies or Institutes for archaeological work in Israel during the seasons of 1959 and 1960.

The above does not include work done on EA and Crusaders' sites, but some interesting sites belonging to these periods were investigated during the decade with which this survey deals.

---

[135]) See above, pp. 13–14; the summary given there is largely based on the results of these excavations.
[136]) See above, p. 35; J. Bowman, B. S. J. Isserlin, K. R. Rowe, Proceedings of the Leeds Philos. Soc. (Lit. and Hist. Section) VIII (1955), pp. 5 ff.
[137]) See above, p. 46.
[138]) B. Bagatti, Liber Annuus V (1955), pp. 5 ff.

## XI. *Conservation of Archaeological Monuments*

The second Division of the Department of Antiquities, which has accomplished a great deal during its existence, is the Division for the Conservation of Monuments. Generations of neglect under the Turks, and to some extent even in the days of the Mandatory Government, have left their mark on the monuments of the past in Israel.

Within the limits of its modest budget, the Department of Antiquities has endeavoured to improve conditions in Jerusalem. Thus, the group of rock-cut tombs dating from the end of the Second Temple period at Sanhedria were cleaned and restored in cooperation with the Ministry of Religious Affairs, the Ministry of Labour, and the Department for the development of Jerusalem, which formerly existed in the Jewish Agency (pl. VII, 1)[139]. The municipality of Jerusalem expropriated most of the land in the vicinity and has transformed the place into a beauty spot. The most monumental tomb was acquired by the Ministry of Religious Affairs from a private owner.

In the winter of 1949–50 the first attempt was made to clear the tomb next to the King David Hotel known as the Tomb of Herod's Family, and to uncover the foundations of the adjacent funerary monument. The immediate vicinity was later improved by the Government Tourist Corporation.

Together with the Department for Christian Communities of the Ministry of Religious Affairs, a considerable area was cleared and fenced in on the hill of John the High Priest, where the remains of two Byzantine churches, one above ground, and one underground, were cleared.

In conjunction with the Department for National Religious Affairs of the Ministry of Religious Affairs, the Jewish synagogue at Shefar'am was cleaned and repaired.

The small Early Turkish monument of Bi'r Zeybak at Lydda has been repaired and restored.

Essential repairs were carried out near the north-west, south-west, and south-east towers of the *khan* (caravanserai) at Rosh Ha'ayin, which were in imminent danger of collapse; and plans are ready to continue the restoration of this *khan*.

The area surrounding the Roman mausoleum at the abandoned village of Mazor was fenced-in and cleared, and a row of trees planted round it. The structure was repaired, and the fenced-in area is being improved now (pl. VII, 2).

Fragmentary mosaic floors from the monastery at Sha'ar Ha'aliyya (Haifa) were transferred on permanent loan to the Municipal Museum of Ancient Art at Haifa. The main mosaic floor from the monastic farm at Bet-Hashshitta was transferred to the Qirya grounds in Jerusalem. One complete mosaic floor from the ruins of a

---

[139]) *Short Guide to the Rock-Cut Tombs of Sanhedriyya* published by the Dept. of Ant., Jerusalem, 1956.

monastery and church at Sede Naḥum was transferred to the campus of the Hebrew University. Three other fragmentary mosaics, to the Museum of the Department. Some mosaics from Ḥanita were restored. The structure above the mosaic at Bet-Govrin was repaired; its main mosaics were removed and repaired, and are now on exhibition at the Museum of the Department. A start was made on the cleansing of the Crusaders' church in the village.

Several other mosaic floors were removed for repairs and will be on exhibition at the Museum of the Dept., while some fragments from Byzantine basilicae at Sukh-mata and Kefar Truman have been given on permanent loan to the Ha'aretz Mu-seum of Tel Aviv; a tomb of the Roman period with coloured frescoes on the walls and vault was repaired and renovated with funds provided by the Local Council of Ascalon. A fragmentary fresco from another Roman tomb was re-moved by Mr. Hevesi, and is now on exhibition at the museum of the Department (pl. VII, 3). A Crusader building at Haifa was cleaned and renovated in cooperation with the municipality. One mosaic floor of the monastery of the Lady Maria at Bet-She'an was repaired, and so was the superstructure covering the whole series of mosaic floors there.

The chief efforts of the Division, however, were devoted to the through-going repair of the mosaics in the ancient synagogue of Bet-'Alpha, which were in danger of falling into ruin. The repairs began in 1949 and were completed in 1957. The entire mosaic has been removed bit by bit from its bed, repaired and replaced in position on a new concrete bed.

In the winter of 1954 the Tourist Centre began an inter-ministerial project for the restoration of historic and religious sites, to help the development of tourism. An inter-ministerial committee was set up, on which were represented the following Ministries: Trade and Industry (Tourist Centre), Education and Culture (Depart-ment of Antiquities), the Treasury, Religious Affairs, Labour and Interior (Town Planning). In Acre the sea-wall, various places in the city-walls, Burj es-Sulṭan, and the so-called Crypt of St. John have been cleaned and repaired. Attention has been paid in Jerusalem to the area round the tomb of Herod's Family and to the column in the quarry at the Police Compound. At Bet-She'an the mosque was turned into a museum. At Bet-'Alpha the building erected over ancient synagogue mosaics has been repaired and the surrounding area tidied. At Caesarea the Sea Gate in the Crusader Wall was repaired, and the areas round the excavations tidied and fenced off. Repairs were accomplished at Bet-She'arim in collaboration with the IES.

None of the work of excavation and preservation listed above would have been possible without the moral and financial support given to the Department of Anti-quities by local authorities, particularly by the municipalities of Tel Aviv, Haifa, Beersheba, Nethanya and Tiberias, and the local council of Ascalon, and by govern-ment and other public institutions. First and foremost among them must be men-

tioned the Ministry of Labour, especially the Housing and Employment Depart-
ments, which latter placed at the Department's disposal thousands of work-days
in various parts of the country.

In 1955 the work of the interministerial committee was taken over by the Government Tourist Corporation, which has since carried out with the approval of the
Dept. of Antiquities cleaning and improvement works on the sites of Megiddo,
Ascalon, 'Avdat ('Abde; pl. VI, 2), and Shivta (Isbeyta). It also completed improvements previously undertaken by the Department at the Tomb of Herod's
Family in Jerusalem, round the ancient synagogue at Kefar Bir'am, where the whole
exterior of the east wall has now been exposed, and is now preparing a detailed
plan for continuing improvements and restorations at 'Akko (Acre), where the
Department of Druze Affairs of the Ministry of Religious Affairs has carried out a
thorough restoration in the Mosque of 'Aḥmed el-Jazzar.

At the same time the Department of Antiquities continued its modest efforts in the
same field in repairing and restoring additional parts of the Mameluk *khan* at Rosh
Ha'ayin, an abandoned early Turkish mosque at Jaljuliyye in the Sharon, the ancient synagogues at Meyron and Kefar Bir'am, repairs of numerous ancient mosaics
(cf., e.g., pls. V, 3; VI, 1), and a gradual restoration and improvement of the monumental tomb of the Hasmonean period at Alfasi St. in Jerusalem[140]), the site of
which was expropriated with the help of the Government Tourist Corporation.

## XII. *Archaeological Inspection*

The rapid progress of development projects and the large number of bodies hand-
ling them, government and semi-government, Jewish Agency, public and private,
made it very difficult to develop a suitable system of inspection, while the limited
staff of the Department prevented the appointment of an adequate number of inspectors. The country is now divided into five zones: the Northern area, comprising
the mountains of upper and lower Galilee, the Ḥule, Jordan, Bet-She'an and Jezreel
Valleys, and Mount Carmel; the Coastal area, extending eastwards to the foothills
in its northern part and the frontier in its southern part, from Rosh Hanniqra to
the Hadera River (Naḥal Ḥadera); the Central area, comprising the Central and
Tel Aviv-Jaffa Districts; the Jerusalem area, comprising the Jerusalem District and
the Ascalon division of the Southern District; the Southern area, comprising the
whole Southern District apart from the Ascalon division.

The inspectors were mainly concerned with answering calls for help from any part
of their areas, whether in connection with the exploration of areas destined for
development, or in connection with the examination of chance discoveries made

---

[140]) See above, p. 6.

in the course of development works such as road-building, laying of railway lines, housing schemes, water-installation, reservoir-digging, etc. Close contacts were established with settlement organizations, and the inspectors, or sometimes other representatives of the Department of Antiquities, participate regularly in the survey and siting committees set up to decide where to place settlements and other agricultural units. In addition to this, all applications for quarrying, mining and drilling wells, as well as plans to develop areas close to or including historic sites, are referred to the Department of Antiquities for inspection or comment. It is often necessary to visit the site in question, in order to find out whether any reservation or stipulation must be made before granting the application or confirming the plan. Such examinations or responses to calls for help have often led to the carrying out of archaeological soundings, and some have subsequently developed into large-scale excavations, as at Bet-Yeraḥ, Tiberias and Caesarea. In all these activities the inspectors received much help from the regional guards[141].

Unfortunately, the pressure of events caused the regular work of the inspectors to be rather neglected, and they were unable fully to discharge such duties as periodical inspection of sites in their areas, and the exploration of their areas to discover new sites. In this last respect, several projects have been partially carried out by the Friends of Antiquities[142], especially partial surveys[143].

## XIII. *Archaeological Museums*

When the Department of Antiquities started to function, it possessed no objects for display to the public. As time went on, finds began to accumulate. They came from various sources: from the Department's own excavations; from the division of finds with expeditions working in Israel; from accidental discoveries; from gifts to the Department; and to a lesser extent from acquisitions from dealers and collectors. In 1949, the Department held two short-term exhibitions, one at Tel Aviv in the early summer, and the other in Jerusalem in the autumn, showing the Department's acquisitions since its foundation, and explaining by means of actual remains, photographs and diagrams the development of material culture in the country from an archaeological point of view.

Only when the Department moved to a somewhat larger building and it became possible to allot a hall and three rooms to the display of antiquities, was the Department's permanent exhibition set up, to serve as the nucleus of Israel's future Archaeological Museum. Mr. Moshe Sharett, then acting Minister of Education and Culture, officially inaugurated the exhibition in a ceremony on July 31st, 1951.

[141] See above, p. 2.
[142] See above, pp. 1–2.
[143] See above, pp. 47 ff.

Later, the whole ground-floor (an additional hall, a corridor and two more rooms) was taken over for exhibition purposes; but the Museum is still very short of space. Plans are being worked out for the erection of an appropriate building to house the Archaeological Museum of the Department.

The exhibition is now open to the public on weekdays, as well as for shorter periods on Saturdays and festivals, when admission is free of charge. 36,291 people have hitherto visited the exhibition; 7,524 of them on days when the admission is free. 15,646 of the visitors were school students, 60% of whom came in organized groups, guided on their visit by especially assigned members of the staff.

In the course of time the Museum arranged several temporary displays on various subjects: New acquisitions (April 1952); excavations of Bet-Yerah (Passover 1953); excavations of Chalcolithic sites in the neighbourhood of Beersheba (1954); survey and excavations in the Hever Valley (Spring 1954); excavations at Nehariyya (August 1954); newly uncovered mosaics (1954); exhibitions of finds from Bet-She‘arim, Ma‘ayan Barukh, Caesarea, Ginnosar, Be’er Matar (1955–6); a special exhibition for the Unesco Museum Week (October 1956); how to arrange an "Archaeological Corner", in connection with the "Days of Study"[144]) (March 1958); opening exhibition in connection with the extension of the Museum (April 1956); fortnightly exhibitions in connection with two series of lectures at the Department of Antiquities on recent excavations (1957/58: Tel Gat, ‘Eynan, Mezer, Tel ‘Ely, the Hasmonean tomb at Alfasi St., Jerusalem; 1958/59: Tel Gat, Kabri and ’Akhziv, ’Azor (LC–EI), Be’er Zafad and ’Azor (Chalcolithic), Kefar Truman and Ruhama, Roglit, Jaffa, Giv‘ataim, Survey of the zone of ‘Adullam); Religion and Cult in Ancient Israel, in connection with the 2nd World Congress of Jewish Studies (July–December 1957); Decade of Archaeology in Israel (May–December 1958).

Two small laboratories are connected with the museum, one for a formatore and the other for a chemist, where pottery, stone and metal objects are restored and cleaned, to prepare them for display and publication.

The Department was not content merely to take care of its central museum, but from the beginning fostered the development of local collections, and regional, and municipal museums. Its policy was to give technical aid and advice on the preparation of rooms and buildings for housing exhibits, as well as to advise on the necessary equipment, furniture, methods of display and explanation of objects. However, an essential condition for opening such institutions was local enthusiasm, i.e. the presence of an enthusiast who originally made the suggestion and took the trouble to work for its realization. Professional advice was frequently given in connection with the acquisition of objects or complete collections, and in most cases public collections and museums were encouraged by the permanent loans of ob-

---

[144]) See below, p. 58.

jects belonging to the Department of Antiquities, which had been found or excavated in the neighbourhood of the museum or the collection in question. Many
objects were also lent for short-time exhibitions held from time to time in such
museums. Since the summer of 1948 municipal museums have been founded at
Haifa, Tel Aviv, Beersheba, Bet-She'an, Tiberias, and Acre. There exists also a
comparatively large number of regional or local collections[145].

During 1953–1955 the Department has been taking care of a large exhibition abroad
– "From the Land of the Bible". Most of the exhibits were shipped from Israel,
some of which were lent by Museums and private collectors; the great majority,
however, were the Department's property. Dr. P. Kahane, Keeper of the Museum
of the Department of Antiquities, was in charge of this exhibition and travelled
with it. The exhibition has been on show in the United States of America (Metro-
politan Museum of Art, New York, 52,000 visitors; the Smithsonian Institute,
Washington, 32,000 visitors; Walters Gallery, Baltimore, Md., 11,500 visitors); in
Great Britain (British Museum, London, 29,000 visitors); in Holland (Municipal
Museum, The Hague, 16,500 visitors), in Sweden (Statens Historiska Museum,
Stockholm, 30,000 visitors), and in Norway (Norsk Folkemuseum, Oslo, 32,000
visitors). The exhibition has been very successful and has been very enthusiastically
and favourably reviewed by the press in these countries. Apart from its educational
value in making real the Bible and Biblical times, the exhibition was a most successful means of presenting the State of Israel and its cultural mission to the general
public abroad.

## XIV. *Archaeological Publications*

The strenuous field-work done by the Department's very small research staff does
not leave them a great deal of time or opportunity to study their finds and prepare
the results of their researches for publication. Nevertheless, some progress has been
made in this field.

In the very first year of its existence, the Department published a Bulletin intended
mainly for the trustees of the Friends of Antiquities. The Bulletin[146] contained
notices by trustees or other interested persons on the discovery of antiquities all
over the country, brief reviews of excavations in progress in Israel and the neighbouring countries, and practical instructions for Trustees.

From time to time, summarizing reports of excavations in Israel are published in
learned periodicals abroad and at home, as well as brief accounts of individual exca-

---

[145] Cf. the list of museums and collections on pp. 60–1.
[146] 'Alon Mahleqet (later 'Agaf) Ha'atiqot, Nos. I–VI (1949–1957).

vations and preliminary reports[147]). Occasional press releases and press conferences are designed to inform the Israel public and (through foreign correspondents) the public abroad of archaeological activities in Israel. Yearly summaries of the work of the Department are published in the Government Year Book (1949–1959). Similar publicity work is being done by the authorities of the Hebrew University and the IES.

The Department has also begun to publish little local guides. A brief guide in Hebrew, English and French to the antiquities at Caesarea has gone through several impressions. Short guides in Hebrew and English have also been published on the excavations at Ramat Raḥel and the Rock-Cut Tombs of Sanhedriyya, at Jerusalem. Guides to Bet-She'an and Megiddo are in preparation. So is a pamphlet on archaeology, in the series of pamphlets for schools issued by the Ministry of Education and Culture. But all this is not enough. The Department needed a periodical publication, in which could be printed both reports on its field activities (excavations, surveys) as well as discussions of new finds, or analyses of classes of objects, and research proper connected with the work done by its staff. The first volume of 'Atiqot (Antiquities), the Department's Journal in Hebrew and English was published in December 1955. The second volume (1959) has been issued, and the third volume is in preparation.

The Department has also initiated a series of popular pamphlets on various classes of antiquities. One, entitled Ancient Pottery of Erez-Yisra'el[148]) (Hebrew and English issues), by Mrs. Ruth Amiran, has already been released. A second issue on Glass[149]), by Dr. P. Kahane, is in preparation. And further issues are planned. Two series of reports on excavations are in preparation. Preliminary reports will start with that of three seasons of work at Tel Gat (now in print), by S. Yeivin. Final reports will be inaugurated with the first volume of Tel Bet-Yeraḥ (now in the final stage of editing) by P. Bar-Adon.

Israel's other archaeological institutions have continued the publication of the results of their researches. Since the death of Professor E. L. Sukenik, the two periodicals published by the Hebrew University Institute of Archaeology have temporarily ceased to appear. They are Qedem and the Bulletin of the Louis M. Rabinowitz Fund for the Exploration of Ancient Synagogues The IES continues to publish its quarterly bulletin Yedi'ot and has started a Hebrew annual 'Erez Yisra'el. So far, five volumes have appeared (1951, 1953, 1954, 1956, 1958). The sixth volume is now in the press. The IES also publishes a quarterly in English, the Israel Exploration Journal, now in its ninth year. Other learned periodicals, such as

---

[147]) A full bibliography by Dr. M. Cassuto-Salsmann on archaeological activity in Israel (up to 1955) was published in Sh. Yeivin, Archaelogical Activities in Israel (1948–1955), pp. 23 ff.; a further up-to-date bibliography by the same author is included in 'Atiqot II (1959), pp. 165 ff.
[148]) Cf. The Holy Land [Antiquity and Survival, II, 2–3, (1957))], pp. 187 ff.
[149]) Cf. P. P. Kahane, Ibid., pp. 208 ff.

Zion, Tarbiz, Yerushalayim, Sinaï, occasionally publish articles on archaeological subjects.

It was a great achievement on the part of the Hebrew University to have acquired in the summer of 1954 the remaining four Dead Sea Scrolls of the group first discovered in a cave near Kh. Qumran. Three were already in its possession. All honour to them who helped to achieve this. All seven scrolls are to be housed in a special "Shrine of the Book" created for the purpose. Recently Dr. Avigad and Yadin published a preliminary volume on the hitherto unopened Aramaic scroll[150]).

## XV.   Epilogue

This survey cannot be concluded without some reference to a serious problem facing all archaeological institutions in Israel, namely the problem of research and technical personnel. True, the Hebrew University Institute of Archaeology and its Department of Prehistory teach and train a young generation of archaeologists from which the Department of Antiquities has drawn a very large proportion of its research workers. But the process of training them, slow enough anywhere, is still slower in Israel, for most University students have to work to support themselves and the period of study is thus unduly prolonged. The Department of Antiquities therefore felt called upon to take extraordinary measures. In the winter of 1951, it arranged an intensive three-months training course for field assistants. The course included lectures and practical work in identifying potsherds, surveying, archaeological drawing and photography. 25 students took the course, among them regional guards and trustees of the Department, and amateurs drawn from the general public. At the end of the course examinations were held. Further three "Days of Study" were arranged for the same public in 1958. Most of the participants now fulfil archaeological functions in the Department and outside of it.

In 1954 a commission of Unesco experts visited Israel at the invitation of the Governement. The chairman was M. Guillaume Gillet, a French architect and townplanner. His job was to advise on the integration of ancient quarters in the planning of modern towns containing them. The second member of the commission was Professor Teodoro Orselli, Director of the Ravenna Academy of Art, whose task was to train technicians in the art of repairing and restoring mosaics and ancient wall-paintings. Mr. A. Hiram, Architect and Conservator of Monuments in the Department of Antiquities and the Israel member of the commission, was its liaison officer and guide, and helped to carry out its work. In the space of four months Prof. Orselli trained about a dozen people in the restoration of mosaics. He also trained a few of these pupils to deal with ancient wall-paintings. Some of

---

150) N. Avigad, Y. Yadin, A Genesis Apocryphon, Jerusalem, 1956.

them are employed today by the Department of Antiquities or are engaged in expeditions of other archaeological institutions[151]).

However, all this is insufficient, and the problem of expert research and technical personnel remains unsolved. It is to be hoped that a joint effort by all archaeological bodies in the country will make possible some progress towards a solution, just as progress has been made in other branches of archaeology, although much remains to be done.

*Jerusalem, March 31, 1959.*

_____

[151]) The report of this mission is being published now by the Israel Department of Antiquities.

## LIST OF ARCHAEOLOGICAL MUSEUMS AND COLLECTIONS
## IN ISRAEL

*Jerusalem*

1. Archaeological Museum, Department of Antiquities, 25, Shelomo Hamme-lekh St.
2. Bezalel National Museum, Shemuel Hannagid St.
3. Museum of Prehistoric Archaeology, Hebrew University, Cremieux St.
4. Archaeological Exhibition, Department of Archaeology, Hebrew University Campus.
5. "Shrine of the Book", exhibition of the Dead Sea Scrolls and ancient manuscripts, Hebrew University Campus.
6. Museum of Antiquities Connected with Religious Customs and Ritual, Chief Rabbinate (Hekhal Shelomo), 58, King George St.
7. The Herbert E. Clark Collection of Near Eastern Antiquities, Y.M.C.A., King David St.
8. Museum of the Pontifical Biblical Institute, Botta St.
9. Schocken Library, 6, Balfour St.

*Tel Aviv*

10. Museum "Ha'aretz", Ramat Aviv.
11. Archaeological-Ethnographic Exhibition "Adam We'amalo".
12. Archaeological Exhibition: Finds from Excavations at Tel Qasile.
13. Archaeological Exhibition, Jaffa – Tel Aviv (to be opened shortly).

*Haifa*

14. Haifa Municipal Museum of Ancient Art, Municipality Building, 14, Hassan Shukry St.
15. Maritime Museum.
16. "Dagon", Batey Mamgurot LeIsrael, Port Area.

*Other Settlements*

17. The Municipal Museum, Acre.
18. Negev Museum, Beersheba.
19. Municipal Archaeological Museum, Bet-She'an.
20. Ussishkin House, Dan.
21. Wilfrid Israel House for Oriental Art and Studies, Hazzorea'.
22. Bet-Hankin, Kefar Yehoshua'.
23. Regional Museum "Yad Labbanim", Petah Tikva.

24. Bet-Zevi, Ramat Gan.
25. Maritime Museum, Sa'ar.
26. Bet Hanna Senes (Caesarea). Sedot-Yam.
27. Museum of Prehistoric Archaeology, Sha'ar Haggolan.
28. Bet Hayim Sturman, Regional Institute of Homecraft, 'Eyn Harod – Tel Yosef.
29. Archaeological Museum, Tiberias.

*Local Collections of Antiquities*

30. 'Alummot (mainly prehistoric archaeology)
31. 'Ayyelet Hashshahar, Bet Zifroni.
32. Barqai.
33. Be'eri.
34. Gat (the collective settlement).
35. Hanita.
36. Huqqoq.
37. Kabri.
38. Kefar Menahem.
39. Kefar Ruppin.
40. Ma'ale Hahammisha.
41. Ma'agan Mikha'el.
42. Ma'ayan Barukh.
43. Ma'oz Hayyim
44. Megiddo (the historic site).
45. Megiddo (the collective settlement).
46. Mezer.
47. Mishmar Ha'emeq.
48. Na'an.
49. Nahshon.
50. Nazareth, The Church of the Announciation.
51. Nehariyya, the building of the Local Council.
52. Nirim.
53. Nizzanim.
54. Revivim (mainly prehistoric archaeology).
55. Sa'sa'.
56. Shamir.
57. Tirat Zevi.
58. Yas'ur.

PLATES

Plate I

1

The Restored Facade of the Catacomb of Sarcophagi at Bet-She⁽arim. (By kindness of Dr. N. Avigad, Director of the IES's Expedition to Bet-She⁽arim).

2

A Set of Three Basalt Bowls from Be'er Matar.

3

Male Bone Statuette from the Chalcolithic Site of Be'er Zafad, near Beersheba. (By kindness of M. J. Perrot, Director of the CNRS's Expedition to Be'er Zafad).

Plate II

1

A Chalcolithic Clay Ossuary from 'Azor, in the shape of a Two-Storeyed Building. (back view.)

2

A Group of Chalcolithic Stone-Vases from Kabri.

3

A Basalt Paved Street in an EC Stratum at Bet-Yerah 'South'.

Plate III

A Modern Cast from an Ancient Mould of a Statuette of 'Atrat-Yam (?) from Nehariyya.

1

A Basalt Lion Orthostat from the Doorway of the Northern LC Temple at Hazor.
(By kindness of Dr. Y. Yadin, Director of the James de Rothschild's Expedition to Hazor).

2

3

4

A Fragment of a Sandstone Doorjamb from the LC Gateway at Jaffa inscribed with the Titles of Ramses II. (By kindness of the Municipality of Tel-Aviv and Dr. Y. Kaplan, the Director of the Excavations).

A Terracotta Figurine from the LI (Persian) Temple near Tell Makmish.

Plate IV

1

The Gateway of the Acropolis at Tel "Gat" in Stratum VIII.
(IXth century B.C.E.). Inside the city.

2

One of the Semi-Detached Columns and
Capitals from the Structure on the Lowest
Terrace of Herod's Palace at Massada. (Photo:
A. Volk.)

Plate V

Part of the Animal Border of the Central Nave in an Open-Air Byzantine Church in the Cemetery of Caesarea.

2

Part of the Mosaic Pavement from the Southern Aisle of a Byzantine Church at Roglit.

3

1

Mutilated Porphyry Statue (Over Life Size) of a Roman Emperor (?) from the Supposed Cattle-Market of the Byzantine Period at Caesarea.

Plate VI

Part of the Mosaic Floor from the Ancient Synagogue at Horvat Ma'on (Nirim).

'Avdat ('Abde) after Cleaning. (Photograph of the Israel Government Press Office).

Plate VII

1

Facade of the Rock-Cut Tomb No. 14 at Sanhedriyya, Jerusalem, First
Century B.C.E. – First Century C. E., after Cleaning.

2

A Roman Mausoleum of the Second-Third Centuries at Mazor
(Maqam en-Nebi' Yiḥye) after Restoration.

3

A Fragmentary Fresco from a Roman Tomb at Ascalon. (Photo:
P. Dorn)